There is no better expert at startup selling than Amos Schwartzfarb. Follow his advice. My success stems from simply telling my startups to listen to Amos's advice on selling. Anyone can sell with a known product, brand, and reputation, but if you want to start the whole process from scratch, you have to listen to Amos Schwartzfarb. You could spend the next decade learning how to sell and not sell through personal experience, or you could just read this book.

—Aziz Gilani, managing director at Mercury Fund

This is a book that all first-time entrepreneurs must read. Getting to repeatable selling in an early-stage company is by far the biggest challenge startups face, and Amos provides an experience-based, prescriptive approach to getting it right the first time. I witnessed the success of Amos's approach firsthand when we built a venture-backed company together and sold it for a 10-times cash-on-cash return.

—Rob Taylor, cofounder and CEO at Convey

I've seen Amos's work at both BlackLocus and with his portfolio at Techstars and can say firsthand that Amos understands how to identify early customers and scale sales organizations. This book should be a go-to for any founder looking to build a business from day one.

—Morgan Flager, general partner at Silverton Partners

Amos imparts valuable insights on hard lessons learned that can apply to any startup founder. He has a very engaging way of presenting practical and inspiring advice to entrepreneurs on how to lead teams, and manage growth, based on his successful track record. This book is for anyone interested in starting, growing, or leading a modern startup.

—John Brown, head of publisher policy
communications at Google

I was fortunate to get to work with Amos while in Techstars Austin. I've seen firsthand how his frameworks and methods impact a company's ability to grow and scale. Reading Sell More Faster *will give you the same unfair advantage we had at ScaleFactor, which has enabled rocket-ship growth in a very short time.* Sell More Faster *is a must-read for every startup CEO and Head of Sales.*

—Kurt Rathmann, founder and CEO at ScaleFactor

During the Techstars accelerator programs, we say "Do more faster." We encourage our portfolio to get product out the door, get early feedback, and iterate quickly. In that phase, the CEO or one of the cofounders typically does all of the selling. This is necessary, as only they can push the whole company to do whatever is needed. In order to do that successfully and set themselves up to scale post-accelerator they need to have product–market direction and be on the road to product–market fit. Sell More Faster *demystifies the complexities on the road to product–market fit and growing a well-run sales organization. A must-read for all startups!*

—David Brown, co-CEO at Techstars

In an industry that tends to obsess about fundraising, finally, there exists the go-to resource focused on the most important part of building and growing a business: sales. I've worked with Amos for years and he has always been the first person I go to for advice for teams who need help with their sales strategy, and now everyone has that access—this book gives everyone the roadmap they need to succeed at growing a scalable sales strategy. Amos Schwartzfarb's approach is so good it feels like cheating.

—Zoe Schlag, managing director at Techstars Impact

Warren Buffett once said, "It's not necessary to do extraordinary things to get extraordinary results." Truer words have never been spoken about achieving success in sales. Amos has held sales leadership positions in a half-dozen companies that had successful exits. That doesn't happen by chance. Working closely with him these past few years, it's easy to see why he's enjoyed success everywhere he's been. While his sunny disposition and genuine love of people have surely contributed, it's clear to me that his adherence to a process is his secret sauce. Over two decades of insight from one of the best sales leaders I've ever been around is tucked in these pages. I'll be giving this book to all the founders I work with.

—Mark Solon, managing partner at Techstars

I've been at Techstars since the early days, and through my own portfolio of investments and through the hundreds of companies I've worked with at Techstars, the one common theme is that every company needs to figure out product–market fit, and then scale sales. Sell More Faster *is a disciplined approach to figuring out who your customers are and how to build a high-performing sales organization. If you're a pre-series A company, this book is a must read!*

—Nicole Glaros, chief investment strategy officer at Techstars

For anyone in sales—which is basically everyone—this book is a must-read. In Sell More Faster, *Amos takes his wealth of experience and translates it into the essential playbook for sales. The real-life stories here are pure gold; the lessons Amos shares were learned on the road. Follow this roadmap to sales success. I'm recommending this book to every startup founder and sales exec that I meet.*

—Anna Barber, managing director of Techstars Los Angeles

This inspiring book provides practical resources and actionable insights for founders. Far too often, content geared toward entrepreneurs is high-level inspiration that merely scratches the surface. As an operator and investor, who has been on both sides, Amos is able to go deeper, tap into the founder mindset, and unpack many of the challenges of scale. This book is an incredible resource and must read for my portfolio companies and students!

—Jenny Fielding, managing director of Techstars New York

When it comes to selling new concepts, Amos is without parallel. Startups and established companies often need to make major pivots in their business. When that happens, you need a talent like Amos who can quickly and successfully sell that new direction to clients.

—Jake Winebaum, serial entrepreneur

Sell More Faster *is the sales playbook every startup founder needs to read. Whether you're searching for product–market fit or have found it and are starting to scale, this book will give you the play-by-play approach of what you need to do to build an awesome sales organization.*

—Brad Feld, partner at Foundry group, cofounder of Techstars

Every company needs to figure out who their customers are and how to scale their sales organization. Sell More Faster *is the first book which takes that complicated task and breaks it down into a playbook every founder can follow.*

—David Cohen, co-CEO of Techstars

Sell More Faster

Sell More Faster

The Ultimate Sales Playbook for Startups

Amos Schwartzfarb

WILEY

Published by John Wiley & Sons, Inc., Hoboken, New Jersey.
Published simultaneously in Canada.

For general information on our other products and services or for technical
support, please contact our Customer Care Department within the United States at
(800) 762-2974, outside the United States at (317) 572-3993 or fax (317) 572-4002.

Wiley publishes in a variety of print and electronic formats and by
print-on-demand. Some material included with standard print versions of this book
may not be included in e-books or in print-on-demand. If this book refers to media
such as a CD or DVD that is not included in the version you purchased, you may
download this material at http://booksupport.wiley.com. For more information
about Wiley products, visit www.wiley.com.

Library of Congress Cataloging-in-Publication Data:

Names: Schwartzfarb, Amos, 1973- author.
Title: Sell more faster : the ultimate sales playbook for startups / Amos
   Schwartzfarb.
Description: First Edition. | Hoboken : Wiley, 2019. | Includes index.
Identifiers: LCCN 2019020019 (print) | LCCN 2019022347 (ebook) | ISBN
   9781119597803 (hardback) | ISBN 9781119597728 (ePDF) | ISBN
   9781119597834 (ePub)
Subjects: LCSH: Selling. | Marketing. | Customer relations. | New business
   enterprises. | BISAC: BUSINESS & ECONOMICS / Sales & Selling. | BUSINESS
   & ECONOMICS / Entrepreneurship.
Classification: LCC HF5438.25 .S5659 2019 (print) | LCC HF5438.25 (ebook)
   | DDC 658.8–dc23
LC record available at https://lccn.loc.gov/2019020019
LC ebook record available at https://lccn.loc.gov/2019022347

Cover Design & Image: © Techstars Central LLC

Printed in the United States of America
V10012407_072319

Dedicated to every founder and entrepreneur who has the courage to pursue their passion and dreams
Also dedicated to my awesome family: Roseann, Sierra, Callie, and Jellie
And finally to my mom for always encouraging me to pursue my dreams and to my dad for teaching me work ethic

Contents

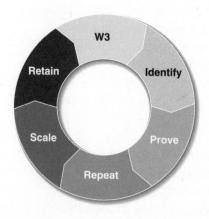

Foreword

From 2005 to 2008, I worked for Amos at Business.com, leading sales teams that sold online advertising. I started with the company in 2001 as an individual contributor when there were just three salespeople and in 2002 was promoted to director and took over the Inside Sales team. My boss gave me quite a bit of latitude, but this was my first *real* sales management role. I used my best judgment to lead sales, but I didn't really know what a "sales strategy" was (and I didn't know that I didn't know). Still, I brought much-needed metrics—orientation, organization, and process—to the team and scaled it out to over 30 sales reps.

That said, it could have been better. We really didn't have a good lead generation strategy because we really didn't know who our high probability targets were or even what our Ideal Customer Profile was. We didn't have a good understanding of how we made money and where we should be selling ads on our site for the most incremental revenue.

Prior to Amos taking over sales and client services, the salespeople could just call on anybody they "felt" would be a good fit for our online advertising products (cost-per-click advertisers, or CPC). For example, it was very easy for a salesperson to go to Overture (formerly goto.com and acquired by Yahoo!) and type in high-value keywords like "web conferencing" or "web hosting" and call on advertisers buying those keywords. It felt like shooting fish in a barrel. But looking at the big picture, we learned that by selling to the upteenth web-hosting advertiser on our site we were merely shifting clicks around, generating very little incremental revenue for our company. It was like shooting fish in a barrel, except it's the same fish you keep hitting over and over.

I remember a great quote by Tiger Woods's former golf coach, Butch Harmon: "If you don't set a target, you'll hit it every time." Yep, we had no target. No specifically articulated idea of who we should be selling to and how we should be generating our target lead lists. So some salespeople would call down lists in local business journals, some would call down Dun & Bradstreet lists, some would call on competitors' customers—calling anybody the salesperson thought would buy and generate revenue for them to hit their quota. We weren't considering if our ads would actually drive new business to our customers, if they could become recurring revenue customers, if their ads would add value to our own site. If they were a reachable business, they became a target. This was incredibly painful. Salespeople would regularly tell me that they'd spend about two hours per day merely doing research to find new advertisers to call that they thought could generate revenue for themselves. Two hours of research each day—this means more than a full day every week *not* selling! That's a tremendous waste of a sales asset.

That's *no strategy*.

But still, by 2005, our company had grown from $225,000 annual revenue to $6 million. I was proud of my team contributions and loved the fact that my boss gave me the leeway to make decisions and be held accountable. Then I heard that my boss was going to take over a different team and that our CEO was bringing in one of his mountain biking buddies ... a guy named Amos from HotJobs.

Who was this new guy? What kind of name was "Amos"? Was my freedom and scope going to end? What was he going to change? As you can imagine, I was nervous about getting a new boss. Sure, things weren't perfect, but the charts were going up and to the right (by hook or by crook) so what was this new guy going to do that *I wasn't*?

And then I watched him take over the sales team and run his W3 playbook. It's really simple ... you can't sell and grow your revenues effectively if you don't know *who* you're selling to, *what* they'll buy, and *why* they'll buy. The simplicity of that framework made it easy for me to follow and makes it easy for any sales leader or entrepreneur to follow to success. I was learning what a *real* sales strategy was. He was teaching me something new ... something that I knew I would be able to use again and again in my future roles. It worked! And it worked *fast*. In a matter of months, the team was moving in a concerted direction because we were operating under a *real* sales strategy for the first time.

From 2005 to 2007, our revenues grew from $6 million to over $60 million annually, and we were acquired by RH Donnelly in 2007 for $345 million. While I had limited sales leadership experience, being a part of implementing this strategy at our company gave me a whole new perspective and helped to shape my future sales leadership opportunities.

And here's the thing: I've since learned that there are a lot of people who preach convoluted, aggressive systems as "sales strategies," but almost all of them fail growing companies and leading teams. However, Amos's system *worked*.

I like to think of this time as *before* W3 and *after* W3, because the impact was so clear. *Before*, sales targeting was a free-for-all. "Call anybody you like," we said. "If you think they'll buy what we're sellin', go for it," we said. So our intrepid sales folks bunkered down in the trenches, pleading with accounts to find something—anything—to sell them, even if it was clear they saw no value in our ad space. There was no time for follow-up or customer development, let alone a funnel that could actually help direct efforts.

Fools!

After, sales targeting became a fine-tuned machine that put precision and accuracy at the top of the pyramid. We had a funnel. We had a process. We actually *thought* about who we needed to talk to and why they would *want* to talk to us. Now we get to tell our valiant sales folks what every smart team wants to hear: "We're giving you the list of *high-probability* prospects who *already buy* cost-per-click advertising and who will *fit into categories* on our site that will *generate the most incremental revenue* for us. It *will* generate this cash because we have a relationship with these customers that's as valuable to us as it is to them: this targeted list of customers buy from us because we can give them a better ROI for their online advertising dollar by delivering higher quality clicks from our niche search engine."

This was transformative because now we had the ability to orchestrate the creation of organized lists for the salespeople based on the strategy that was best for the business, which fueled our segmentation and lead prioritization strategies for the whole sales team; and everyone made more money.

By following this simple approach, we went from throwing pasta at a wall to orchestrating a lavish dinner party so desirable that R.H. Donnelly wanted to pay $345 million for a seat at the table. Those who were part of the leadership team went on to start their own companies, lead $500 million sales teams at Viacom/MTV, and take other Los Angeles startups from nothing to millions. But for me, the most important lesson learned was what a real sales strategy consisted of. I took his approach to my opportunities and repeated the playbook with success. I've used the W3 approach when I started my own business in Sales Strategy and Recruiting and while at ZipRecruiter, where I grew the sales team from two salespeople to over 400 in less than six years.

What this strategy did for us at Business.com and what it continues to do for anyone who uses it is simple, but important: it personalizes the sales process. As a CEO, founder, sales leader, or up-and-coming sales rep just trying to gain a foothold, it's easy to focus so much on the numbers and the selling that you can grow blinders to the most critical person in the process: the customer. They don't have to buy what you are selling, so you have to know why they will benefit from it. You have to know where they exist and what they're worried about. And having that simple—but solid—formula to ask *who*, *what*, and *why* helps center the sales and growth process so that companies and customers can thrive.

—Kevin Gaither
SVP of sales at ZipRecruiter
March 2019

Acknowledgments

I've been looking forward to writing this section since I wrote the first chapter because I know this book would not have been possible without the love and support of so many people. If I have missed anyone, it wasn't on purpose, so please call me out!

I have to start with my family. Thank you to my wife, Roseann, who had to deal with my self-centered focus during this process (and always). I do know just how singularly focused I can be; thank you for both sticking by my side and also giving me the space to write and think. I also want to thank my daughters Sierra and Callie—so much of my motivation comes from wanting you to be proud of your papa and so that you can look at me with the same admiration that I feel for you. I love you all.

As for my mom and dad, I can make a long list because without them I wouldn't be here, but instead I'll distill it down to this—for my mom, when I was in ninth grade you once asked me if I was afraid to win. I never forgot those words and they have inspired me every day of my life. For my dad, in my eyes you are the epitome of overcoming the odds through work ethic and sheer force. You've set an example for me my entire life that I'll never be able to repay. And my sisters, Jessie and Sara, have been by my side and in my heart every day of my life, even when I am a self-absorbed and absentee brother. Y'all rock!

Thanks to John Wiley & Sons, and specifically my editor, Christen Thompson, who believed in me, worked with me as a teammate even before day 1, and has been the perfect balance of supportive and informative throughout the process. I thank Vicki Adang on the editing team, who worked tirelessly to make sure that we put out an awesome book.

David Cohen, David Brown, and Brad Feld: you've been incredible from the day I reached out to you for some help and guidance. You've never hesitated to open your experience to me and help me figure out what I'm doing. And I'm forever grateful for the opportunity to make *Sell More Faster* a part of Techstars' history.

My local team in Austin—Zoe Schlag, Trevor Boehm, and Christine DiPietro—getting to the finish line would not have been possible without your support. Thanks to Zoe—I knew I could always count on you to help make sure we weren't dropping (too many) balls. Thanks to Christine, for not only always, always, always having my back but also for making sure everything else was running smoothly and for helping with editing. And thanks to Trevor for so much, but more than anything for giving me confidence when I hit moments of doubt.

Next I want to thank all of the contributors you'll hear from in this book. In no particular order, thanks to: Noah Spirakus, Kurt Rathmann, Al Ismali, Troy Henikoff, David Brown, Russell Foltz-Smith, Monica Landers, AJ Bruno, Jenny Lawton, David Loia, Kalyn Blacklock, Deepak Sekar, Hersh Tapadia, Jason Thompson, Chris Richter, Autumn Manning, and Michael Gilroy, I really appreciate you taking the time out of your busy schedules to contribute to *Sell More Faster*. The book is significantly better because of your experience and contributions.

Thanks to Kevin Gaither, not only for your contributions to the book but also for being an integral part of W3 at Business.com and being my go-to sales expert since those days. To Rob Taylor, not only for your contributions but also for trusting my process in the early days of BlackLocus and for continuing to support me years later. To Guy Goldstein, founder and CEO of WriterDuet, the platform I used to write *Sell More Faster*. To Austin Dressen for 100% of the artwork in the book. To Pete Birkeland for all the notes, advice, and edits along the way—you as much as anyone know how far this has come.

Along the way, there were several people who read early versions when this was just a series of blog posts, helped me build confidence that there was a book inside me, and offered awesome advice and guidance on how to pull it out: Nicole Glaros, Jason Seats, Trevor Boehm, Troy Henikoff, Nadine Kavanaugh, Christine DiPietro, Zoe Schlag, and Andy Aguiluz—thank you so much.

Over the past 24 years, I've worked with some amazing people who, whether they know it or not, have played a crucial part in helping me create the content for this book. Without these people, the content of this book wouldn't be possible. Thank you to Jake Winebaum (Work.com, Business.com, and beyond); Richard Johnson (Hotjobs); Dave Carvajal (HotJobs); Tom Shores (Shoreline Mountain Products); Lordes Colon and Irene Monzon (Bravo Group); Chris Bloch and Rowan Jimenez (Cityrock); AJ Johnson, Scott Shepard, and Maria Callahan (HotJobs); Brian Barnum, Dan Machock, Tonia Weisner and Mark Mazzei (business.com), Stacy Horne (from college to mySpoonful and beyond); Dan Cohen (mySpoonful); Denis O'dwyer (starting at Hotjobs and never ending); Rob Taylor (starting at Blacklocus and never ending); Lukas Bouvrie and Chris Richter (BlackLocus); Morgan Flager (BlackLocus and beyond); Aziz Gilani (BlackLocus and beyond); Tim Gray and John Christiano (Joust); Alex Reiss and Ali Blasco (HotJobs, Utopia, and motivating beyond words); John Fein (Firebrand Ventures); Michael Sidgmore (several coinvestments and an example for how all humans should behave); Ryan Broshar and Natty Zola (Matchstick Ventures); Cody Simms (Techstars and well beyond); David Mandell (Techstars and beyond); and last, but certainly not least, my brother from another mother, Mark Solon, for reminding me who I am and helping me be who I want to be.

Thank you to every company in my Techstars portfolio who believed in me and Techstars and has allowed us to work with you to build great businesses.

To my D&C crew—Solon, Flo, Seats, Glaros, Broshar, Natty, Cam, Cody, and Mandell—the love you all bring to this world, the intellect you share, the warmth and comfort you all impart to everyone in your path is infectious and you are all examples of the beauty in humanity. You make the world two-and-a-half times a better place!

Anyone who knows me also knows my love for all music. I'd be remiss if I didn't acknowledge the music that got me through the writing of *Sell More Faster*. While working on this book I had two albums that I listened to on repeat: the live Grateful Dead album,

Pacific Northwest '73–'74: Believe It If You Need It—the combination of rockin' tunes and great jams helped me get my brain onto paper. And the driving distortion from the Willowz album *Talk in Circles* got me through marathon editing sessions.

Finally, to all of my readers: starting a business is hard and scary, and without you this book wouldn't be possible. I know you have a long road ahead. Thanks for believing in me and for using *Sell More Faster* as a guide to help you win.

Introduction: *Sell More Faster*—Why You Need to Read This Book

> *There are two activities in business, and only two. You are making stuff or you are selling stuff. And no one gets to make stuff if they can't at least sell themselves as someone who can make stuff someone else can sell. So really, there's only one main activity in business, selling stuff. Amos does this activity better than anyone I've worked with. At the end of the day there's a scoreboard and Amos has run up the score in several business categories—focusing on the one main activity.* Sell More Faster *is your fast track to learning how to sell the stuff you want to make.*
> —Russell (Russ) Foltz-Smith, artist, mathematician, technician, educator, and serial entrepreneur

In order to survive, every company in the world has to figure out sales. Sales is everything, from who your customer is to your sales process to scaling your team and servicing your customers. There have been hundreds—if not thousands—of books written about different aspects of sales. While books exist for everything from sales philosophy to process and methodologies, there is not a real playbook for startups to figure out how to build a long-term, highly profitable, and efficient sales organization from day one.

I decided to write it.

I've been working in, founding and investing in startups since 1997, always in some sort of sales capacity. My experience over the past two decades has led to dozens of weekly requests to help CEOs, sales leaders, and startups figure out how to overcome their challenges in sales. And as the managing director at Techstars Austin, a startup accelerator with a mission to help entrepreneurs succeed, every year several of my peers have asked if I'd come in and give a sales workshop.

I had never written anything down formally but decided to outline what a series of workshops might look like. As I got deeper into it, I came up with 18 potential workshops that I ultimately turned into a six-part blog series meant to help Techstars founders (and really anyone) figure out how to start and build their sales organization. And with that, both Techstars and John Wiley & Sons signed on and gave me the opportunity to write *Sell More Faster* and share this time-tested methodology with you!

To get the most out of my process, you'll need to take the time to learn not only from my experiences but from the collective wins and losses of other successful founders and startup sales leaders as well. Woven into this book are stories and commentaries from founders and early stage sales leaders I've worked with over the years.

I call this system the W3 Method: *Who* are you selling to, *What* are they buying, and *Why* do they buy it? Seems simple, right? It is, but it's also hard to keep sight of and (thankfully) easy to come back to when you're lost.

Some of the steps presented in this book may feel tedious, small, or slow; and they are, when practiced in a vacuum. But they are foundational to experimenting and proving what you are building, and they are crucial to building a world-class, successful sales organization. These concepts will help you avoid common pitfalls that *really* slow down your ability to scale fast, and often can even kill your startup. They will also give you the tools to articulate to your teams, customers, and investors *what* you are doing and *why* it works.

Keep this simple concept in mind: *Instinct drives vision and data sets direction.*

Ponder that for a minute. The typical founder mindset is barging ahead with passion, armed with gut instincts. While this frame of mind is crucial for founders to succeed, channeling that energy into a disciplined focus will help produce greater results on a faster timeline. At the times when you try to rush through an exercise or question it, ask yourself if you really have enough data to move forward or if you just want to believe you do simply so you can move faster.

Starting Up

I've been a part of seven startups over the past 23 years. Five of those have exited for over $850 million. The sixth is still teetering along and the seventh company is Techstars (at least, it was a startup when I joined as Austin's managing director in 2015). Until Techstars, I had never joined a startup with more than 20 employees and I was usually one of the first five (or the founder). Techstars was closer to 100 employees when I joined, but I was still present in the earlier part of our amazing growth curve.

When I first moved to San Francisco in 1993, I would have laughed if you asked if I were an entrepreneur or a sales person. Unlike many people today (and even back then), it wasn't the booming tech scene that brought me there: for me it was the history, the rock climbing, the proximity to Yosemite, and the Grateful Dead. Yet, when I think back on those early days, I can see the beginning of my path peeking through with this commonality: venturing into the unknown with not enough money, an unclear path, and the notion that in order to make money I needed to provide value to someone, somewhere—sound familiar?

Shoreline Mountain Products

In 1997, I got a job at Shoreline Mountain Products, a company you have likely never heard of. Shoreline Mountain Products was a mail order company that sold rock climbing gear. This was before the internet was prevalent and before e-commerce was a thing. Instead, our main sales channel was through a 100-plus page paper catalogue that we mailed twice a year to a list we purchased of people who rock climb. When I joined, there were three of us working out of Tom Shores's living room and garage (the makeshift warehouse), answering phones and packing boxes. Four months into my work at Shoreline Mountain Products, I was on the phone with a friend of mine, Alexis Rodriguez. Alexis had recently founded the digital agency Raw Interactive. Alexis asked me if we had thought about creating an online presence and selling gear on the internet.

I suggested this to Tom and he was all in. I have to hand it to him: first, for really understanding who his customers were, and who they were going to be (which was younger and more afflu-ent climbers); and second, for having the courage to experiment. Those two things are important and you will hear them over and over in different ways throughout this entire book.

With Alexis's help we launched a very crude e-commerce site in the summer of 1997. The rest was history. Ultimately Shore-line Mountain Products sold to Mountain Gear—at the time REI's biggest regional competitor—which resulted in Mountain Gear having an e-commerce experience before REI!

> *Lessons learned*: Starting a business wasn't like turning on a light switch. You can't just decide to do it and the customers will come. It required lots of hard work to be successful, both physical and mental. It required figuring out who our customers were and what they wanted. It also required con-stant innovation to stay relevant. We touch on these topics in Chapters 2, 3 and 7.

HotJobs.com

In 1999 I joined HotJobs.com after a chance meeting with one of the founders, Dave Carvajal. HotJobs was one of the original online job boards and a leader in the space. I was one of the first 20 salespeople in our San Francisco office. The company was headquartered in New York, had fewer than 50 employees, was doing less than $10 million in revenue, and was private. Three months after I joined, we had an initial public offering (IPO). This all happened in the middle of the internet boom, through the infamous internet dot-com bubble of 2000, and into the rebound through 2004.

I was at HotJobs for about four and a half years and in that time I touched on almost every aspect of the sales organization. I was a salesperson, ran an inside sales team, built out and scaled the account management team, and created both our first Winback program and our renewal process before being acquired by Yahoo! Then, inside Yahoo!, I helped rebuild a regional sales team, and then moved over to help build out both account management and part of sales for the newly formed strategic accounts division.

I reflect back on my time at HotJobs as my hands-on MBA. The list of things I learned are probably a book all by themselves, but there are two things that stand out when it comes to figuring out how to sell more faster:

Lessons learned

1. In order to have a long-lasting and successful business, you must provide a value to your customer that is obvious, measurable, and irreplaceable. And while this may seem obvious, I see hundreds of businesses a year that not only don't do this, but the founders don't even think about what that means for their customers. At HotJobs, we did this so well that we were recession-proof. When the bubble did burst in 2000, our revenue and customer base continued to grow. We touch on this in Chapters 3 and 5.

2. Culture matters, people matter, and it starts at the top. I remember thinking I'd never work in such an amazing culture again because it was so infectious. Especially in those pre-Yahoo! days, *everyone* was drinking the Kool-Aid. This is all because of the great culture and leadership set by our founding CEO, Richard Johnson, and because of the maniacal focus on hiring the right people by our founding sales recruiter Dave Carvajal. When you can build teams and a company of people who deeply believe in your vision, and when you are the kind of leader whom people want to follow into the fire, your chance of building a successful company increases exponentially. When I joined HotJobs there were dozens of competitors and we were not one of the leaders, but because of Richard's leadership, the culture he built, and the incredible people at HotJobs, by the time we were acquired by Yahoo!, HotJobs was one of the top two job boards as measured by both traffic and revenue. We dig into culture in Chapters 6 and 7.

Work.com and Business.com

In 2004, after leaving Yahoo!HotJobs, I founded Work.com with Jake Winebaum and Russell Foltz-Smith. Work.com was incubated inside Business.com and essentially was an early version of what

Indeed is today. Jake and I eventually decided to merge the two companies together and double down on Business.com. I took over inside sales first and eventually all of sales and client services for Business.com. When I first took over sales in late 2005, we were under $10 million in annual revenue and by the time I left, after being acquired by R.H. Donnelly in 2007, we were at $70 million annually.

During my time at Business.com is when all the learning from Shoreline Mountain Products and HotJobs.com started to resonate with me. I developed a framework called W3, which is the foundation I now use to build any sales organization. It's also the entirety of Chapter 1.

While I've continued to learn (a lot) since the Business.com days, it was then that the concepts of *Sell More Faster* were first forming. At Business.com, we figured how to grow revenue, scale the organization, reduce churn to almost zero, create an infectious culture and achieve rocket ship type growth, all within 18 months. If HotJobs was my MBA, then business.com was my PhD.

> *Lessons learned*: So many lessons! But, most important, having a clearly defined idea of your customers and the value you provide is not only important to acquire new customers, but crucial to building a great culture, attracting awesome investors, and building a world class company. We will be jumping right into the W3 framework in Chapter 1.

MySpoonful

In 2008, I founded MySpoonful with Stacy Horne. MySpoonful was a thrice weekly email newsletter that delivered curated, up-and-coming bands to your inbox. We bootstrapped MySpoonful for four years and built a large and engaged user base. Revenue was always modest and barely covered our costs, but even so we were approached and eventually sold the company to another company that brokers music rights.

> *Lessons learned*: Again, I learned a tremendous amount at MySpoonful, but the biggest lesson I learned was that finding the value that your customers see in your product

(not the value that you think they should see) is crucial to identifying who your customers are. We talk about this in Chapters 2, 4, and 7.

BlackLocus

In 2012 I was living in Austin and was introduced to Rob Taylor, CEO of BlackLocus. I joined him as head of sales. BlackLocus provided intelligence and analytics to online retailers, specifically based on price and assortment. When I joined, BlackLocus believed their customers were small online retailers and Amazon sellers who were trying to compete with big retailers. In the first few months I questioned everything. We quickly learned that the initial hypothesis regarding our customer was wrong, and using the concepts in this book figured out how to flip it to a very different group: enterprise retailers. Seven months later we went from virtually zero revenue to over $120,000 in monthly recurring revenue (MRR) and shortly after sold the company to one of our customers, TheHomeDepot, for over $50 million.

> *Lessons learned:* While it was a quick journey, BlackLocus was where I really put all my past learnings to work. And again, while there was so much to learn, my biggest takeaway was that W3 works as a framework to identify what your business is and how to grow it. BlackLocus is where I most deliberately put all the concepts of this book into practice and the result was the fastest trajectory to high sales growth and acquisition I've experienced (as both an operator and investor).

Joust

In 2013 I founded Joust with Tim Gray and John Christiano. Joust was a consumer app, innovating on the daily fantasy trend and bringing it to "anything." After the fast and large exit with BlackLocus, I was feeling invincible. We were able to get some really early and big interest, signing up customers like XGames, MTV, Discovery Channel, Fox Sports, and more before we had a fully developed product. Ultimately we were not able to build a successful company at Joust, despite the early excitement from these big brands, and I left 36 months later.

You've heard it from founders and VCs alike and it's true, you can learn as much, if not more, from failing as you can from succeeding. And for me, the beauty of this failure is that it was really the final nail in helping me to solidify my core beliefs in how to build a big and successful business. And while there are literally dozens of things I learned at Joust, here are the three most relevant for this book.

Lessons learned

1. If you try to go wide in who you are selling to or try to provide service to too many customer types, you end up providing minimal value to all and maximum value to none. Not only did we have two customer types (media companies and individual consumers) who had competing interests, we also tried to service every profile-user type and media company type. As a startup, it was way too much to try and figure out how to make everyone feel value when there were so many customer types we were trying to serve. We discuss this in Chapters 2, 3, and 7.
2. If you don't know why and can't measure the value your customer is getting from your product, neither can they – and without a clear identification of that ongoing value, your customers will go away. We didn't spend enough time trying to learn this, and there were just too many customer types. This is at the core of why we failed. We cover this in Chapters 2, 4, and 7.
3. Ego doesn't win and hard work alone isn't enough. You need a framework, a methodology, and data to work from in order to test, learn, and refine your process. The three founders of Joust all thought we could figure it out simply by working hard because we'd "done it before." We ignored the basic fundamentals, outlined in *Sell More Faster* and ultimately were not successful. It took us three years and $1.5 million to figure that out. And while we may have still failed, even if we did follow the concepts in this book, we would have failed much faster and much cheaper.

Techstars

This brings me to the summer of 2015 when I became managing director of the Techstars Austin Accelerator. Since joining Techstars I've invested in and worked with 40 companies via the accelerator and have mentored another 100-plus through both Techstars and various angel investments. This means I have put this framework into play time and time again and have witnessed how it helps companies like Chowbotics, ScaleFactor, Storyfit, Prospectify, Helper Bees, Allstacks, Skipper, Mesur, DocStation, Transmute, WriterDuet (the platform where this book was written), and many more scale from virtually zero revenue to millions. This framework has also made it clear when a business was not scaleable and a pivot was needed.

The pieces have been there and go as far back as my days at Shoreline Mountain Products, but it wasn't until recently that I was inspired to write this book.

About This Book

In the coming pages, along with the broader lessons, I've included real-life examples of how these principles have worked for me. The book contains seven chapters that will provide frameworks that begin with figuring out a path from identifying product–market fit to how you test your theories to the building and scaling of your sales organization, ending with what happens after the sale is closed and you have customers. This book is meant to be an operational playbook starting on day one.

I've also solicited friends and colleagues to share their stories as they relate to these principles. You'll hear real-life examples of these ideas and concepts in action and how they worked in specific cases. I've also included a few exercises at the end of some chapters so that you can apply these principles directly to your business as you are reading.

I feel very fortunate for the journey I've been on since Shoreline Mountain Products and for the opportunity to work with so many amazing founders each year through Techstars. My biggest hope with this book is that you, the startup founder, can avoid common mistakes and figure out, as quickly as possible, how to build and scale a world-class company.

I really hope that you enjoy reading it and find it useful. And I have a request of you. Send me feedback to amos@sellmore fasterbook.com. I want to hear what works, what doesn't, and what you might do differently. Feedback can be when you read it or months (or years) later after you've applied these principles. Help me continue to make this better so future CEOs and companies can benefit from our collective learnings.

Thank you for reading and I look forward to hearing how *Sell More Faster* has helped your company grow!

Chapter 1

The W3 (Who, What, and Why) Framework

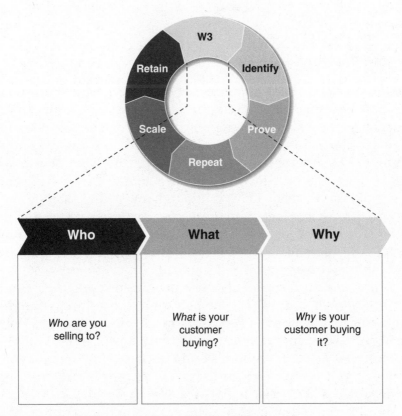

Figure 1.1   The W3 Framework (Who, What, and Why)

At the start of Techstars 2017 program, I remember proudly announcing each KPI meeting that "Sales were great this week … and we have no idea why." Amos constantly reminded us that we needed to know the triggers of our business to have any control over our growth trajectory. We ultimately realized the answer to the 3Ws was the missing ingredient, and explained exactly what was preventing our company from massive scaling: we had achieved product market fit only among super-users in a niche market. We had a false sense of confidence because it took no effort to sell to our (few) optimal users, but it was extremely difficult to sell to anyone else.

—Guy Goldstein, founder and CEO of WriterDuet

Where the Heck Do I Start?

No business can exist without paying customers, which means no business can exist without sales. It's relatively easy to look at any company, especially one doing well, and be able to describe who their customers are. However, when you are first building your business all you have is a theory of *who* you think your customer will be, based on your theory of the problem you are solving and your opinion of what you want to sell them. While it's important for you to have a strong point of view to get started, it's even more important to figure out if you are right before you get too far along. The repercussions of being wrong can be very expensive and can even cause your business to fail.

We've all heard stories about companies pivoting their product or customer focus. I've personally witnessed it dozens of times while working at startups and now with Techstars Austin. Pivots, small and large, are often crucial to figuring out how to build a big business; however, without a framework to figure out *who* your customer is, *what* they are buying, and *why* they buy it, ensuring your success is like trying to find a needle in a haystack.

In this chapter we'll discuss the W3 Framework (Figure 1.1). This is what I used at Business.com, mySpoonful, and Black Locus. It's also the framework I encourage my portfolio companies at Techstars to use. I've broken this chapter into five parts to make it a little more digestible.

This section is a description of W3, the framework I recommend identifying your ideal customer profile (ICP) and why it's important to start this work early on. In the second, third, and fourth sections, we'll dig into each of the three Ws.

"*Who*" Are You Selling To? explores identifying the *who*—who you believe your customer is and how you go about validating it.

In "*What*" Is Your Customer Buying? we will dig into the *what*, meaning what product or service you are selling (compared to what the customer is actually buying). Likewise, we will explore how you can validate that you are selling the right product to the right buyer.

And finally, in "*Why*" Is Your Customer Buying It? we will discuss the *why* of your business—*why* your customer is buying your product and *how* your customer will measure the impact on their business.

In the fifth section "Putting W3 Together," I'll present you with an in-depth exercise to help you thoroughly outline your sales plan.

* * *

Startup founders, especially in early-stage companies, often develop their sales plan based on their personal (and hopefully deep) understanding of the problem they are trying to solve and the product they are bringing to market. However, in my experience, most founders are not great at articulating exactly what they're doing or why. Founders may have a strong idea regarding who their customers will be and what their product or service will be. But in most cases, very little is done to validate their theory and even less is done to capture it in a way that is easy for anyone to comprehend. In the early days of starting your company when you are the one selling to customers, this is fine. However, this immediately becomes a problem when you start trying to hire, forecast, and raise money. The problem with not having an articulated sales plan is that you leave employees, candidates, investors, and even potential customers guessing at who buys what and why, and this, in turn, results in a lack of alignment, clarity, and confidence in the future of your business.

I've now been running sales organizations for over 20 years. Early on, I too failed to understand the importance of a clearly articulated sales plan. In fact, the concept of taking the time to articulate and write down a formal plan seemed like a giant waste of time. Worse, if what we were doing and why we were doing it wasn't obvious to someone, I questioned their intelligence or commitment to the company.

I was wrong.

At that point in my career, I hadn't been around enough experienced leaders building real (and big) companies to understand the importance of planning and process. I also didn't have (or even understand why I should have) mentors to help me grow. This was all on me to figure out. The good news was, my parents were both excellent role models for my strong work ethic. They had a keen and insightful worldview and taught me early on how to think about the present, but also about how events of today will affect the future. I've always had good intuition when it comes to business and over the years I've learned to trust my gut (and I could write an entirely different book on that). What I lacked was anyone ever showing me how to connect the dots from what was in my head and translating that into a plan to build something amazing.

Connecting the Dots from Thoughts to a Plan

In 2005 I was recently promoted to run sales and client services for Business.com. I finally realized just how important it was to articulate what "our" plan was—and why it was that way.

Business.com was an earlier-stage company poised for huge growth but had not arrived there yet. We had around 70 employees, in the mid-seven digits of revenue, and were selling a business-to-business (B2B) search product in the early days of Google Adwords. My predecessor did an incredible job getting us to that point and when his role evolved to focus more on corporate and business development, I was asked to step in for the next iteration of scaling our sales organization.

By this point we had a very experienced leadership team made up of ex-Yahoo, eBay, and Careerbuilder execs and a seasoned board made up of partners, founders, and CEOs from Benchmark, IVP, Earthlink, Boingo, shopping.com, PayPal, and LowerMyBills. While I had great intuition on developing a plan and some raw talent at sales, I had very little classical business training (i.e. no MBA and to this point no great mentor to teach me). It wasn't until I was asked to present my vision to the board that I truly realized the importance of defining and articulating a sales plan.

Fortunately my CEO, Jake Winebaum, was (and still is) an incredible strategist and likewise very good at cultivating raw talent. He wouldn't let me present anything less than a world-class plan and pushed me very hard to develop and articulate mine—this is where I truly learned the importance of taking what was in my head (and gut) and putting it on paper for everyone in the organization to see.

The best way for me to describe to you the weeks of intense mental work I put into developing this plan is to tell you about Jake's ability to ask one simple question: *Why?* Jake asked me "*Why* do you believe this to be true?" at every stage and about every aspect of the plan as it evolved. Multiple times a week I'd be in his office sharing the next iteration of the plan, and week after week I'd leave asking myself the same questions he was asking me. At times this was frustrating and borderline infuriating because I really never had anyone question or push me to that level of detail and specificity in the past, but ultimately it was one of the most valuable experiences I've had as a professional (and one I've carried forward with my work at Techstars).

What it forced me to do was dig inside my instincts and look for opinions, facts, and data to support what my gut was telling me. Sometimes that would help me support my opinion and other times it helped me to see potential flaws and areas of risk. Ultimately, it gave me (and him) the confidence to present the plan to the board and eventually the entire company because we knew we had something that we can easily articulate to anyone, the data to support the direction, and an understanding of the areas of risk.

I called my plan W3, which stood for *who, what,* and *why.* I presented it to the board and executive peers. They all bought in. Then I rolled it out to the sales team, making sure that everyone grasped both what we were doing and why. The result was amazing. Immediately we saw alignment across the entire sales team and across the company, which contributed to massive revenue growth (mid-seven to mid-eight digits) over the next 18 months, and eventually a sale of the company to R.H. Donnelly for $345 million.

Required: A Solid Sales Plan

I want to take some time to describe the alignment and why that was so important. It's not that Business.com didn't have a clear vision; we did. We were also fortunate in that we had a healthy culture of people who loved the company, loved the mission, and believed in Jake as CEO (and the rest of the leadership team, as well). What we lacked was alignment in how to grow our sales in a meaningful way. Sales reps had little direction regarding what was best for the business versus what was best for their commission (or that those two things could be aligned). Also, while our product and marketing teams were very strong, there was virtually no alignment on how product, marketing, and sales all informed each other in a way to accelerate growth. What W3 did for Business .com was to bring all of the pieces together around common language and mission so that we all had a strong sense of how to work together and build a very big company.

That experience was incredible in terms of helping me understand how to build a big and valuable business. More specifically, I learned that in order to have a working, growing, and effective sales department (and company) you *need* a well-defined and articulated sales plan. This is not a suggestion: it is a requirement. Having a strong plan that the entire team can believe in and get behind drives sustainable results.

So what is W3 and how can you use it to build and grow your sales organization? W3 is a framework for developing your plan. It stands for the three most important attributes of a sale: *Who* are you selling to? *What* are they buying? and *Why* are they buying it?

In the next three parts, we will dive into each W separately. Some of this may seem really obvious while other parts could feel tedious. I'm sharing this with you in advance because I want you to be prepared for taking the time to put in the work. This will be the foundation both for everything else in this book and more important to helping you figure out how to build a great sales organization and incredible company.

Who Are You Selling To?

If you don't know your WHO, your WHO becomes everyone. This means engineering becomes swamped with features to make anyone/everyone happy. Sales can't build repeatability; marketing has to build a message that resonates with everyone. Targeting everyone means you become the best for no-one. Your WHO aligns your company's teams, and gives you the ability to focus and execute in a single direction.
—Noah Spirakus, founder and CEO of Prospectify

Who are you selling to? What is your target industry? What segment(s) will get the most value? How do you identify and prioritize targets? Who is the target buyer within each company? What is the job title of the typical buyer? How do we know we are right?

These are just a few of the questions you will start to answer as we go through this section. It's at this point that you may be saying to yourself, "I know who my customer is" and feel that you can skip this. Pause. Ask yourself why you believe that. What is the reason you believe you know who your target customer is, and what data do you have to support your theory? To what level of granularity can you describe your target customer? What can you do to prove you are right (or prove you are wrong)? Can everyone in your company describe, specifically, *who* your target customer is?

I know there are a lot of questions here. Remember when I said this might feel tedious? This is the time to open up your laptop (leave your email and iMessage closed) and start answering these questions (writing down any new ones that pop up).

Before we do that, I want to talk more about how we will approach defining *who*. My experience shows that most startup CEOs (and even many startup sales leaders) can quickly describe the high-level version of WHO they believe their customer is but stop there. Let's use Transmute, one of my portfolio companies, as an example. Transmute has created a new identity protection and management platform using blockchain technology. While this product could potentially help any company of any size, in this example the CEO has already narrowed down their target customer. When Transmute entered Techstars, if you asked the

CEO who their customers are, she would have responded, "We sell to enterprises."

This was a good start. They had already cut out a huge number of potential customers where they will not spend their time selling, but what kind of enterprise is Transmute targeting? She could have meant software, retail, healthcare.

She may define enterprise as a company with above a specific number of employees or revenue threshold. If I'm trying to help this company, I'm still not sure where to start.

My next question for this CEO was, "What type of enterprise?" The CEO was able to take it a step further and say, "We sell to enterprises in the healthcare space." This was a better start as it plants a flag in the ground, but there is still a lot more work to do. I still wasn't sure if they meant hospitals or software companies selling into hospitals or medical device companies or something else. I was also unsure of who I could contact inside that company who cares about the problem that their product solves.

It's likely you've gotten to this level of granularity, and maybe even a little further. At this point, you have two more jobs:

- Get more granular
- Disprove it

Job 1: Get More Granular

This is a conversation I have with every single founder I invest in, and the conversations are often heated. What I will assert is that you want to define the narrowest and most specific customer type that you can in the beginning. Here is an example of how Transmute could think about it to ultimately identify their target customer, "We sell to enterprises in the healthcare space. These are private hospitals with over 5,000 employees. Those hospitals currently have two specific legacy products focused on patient identity protection and have had a breach in the past 90 days. The buyer in those hospitals typically has the title of director of security and information."

Take a minute to notice what we did here. We took an important directional flag indicating who we believed our customer to be and formed an opinion about a much narrower potential customer type. This is often where I start getting pushback, specifically the retort, "This is too narrow and will limit my ability to build a huge company. Investors won't see the potential scale and our sales team will feel too limited in making commissions."

While on the surface this may feel true, it's actually the opposite. Keep in mind that right now all you have is a strong belief of who your customer might be and not enough data to prove it.

By defining the narrowest possible group of customers, what you are actually doing is starting to build out a case, using data, that there is a definable group who *does* buy your product and can't live without it. This is critical in any stage of your business but especially in the earliest stages where all you have are theories. And while it might feel like you are limiting your growth potential, what you are actually doing is building your business around exactly the right customers to buy your product. These customers will inform how your product evolves as well as giving you more data on who the next set of customers could be. They also become the case studies and proof points that you can point to that show that your product works and brings value to your existing customers. Or, you'll quickly learn that this is *not* meant to be your target customer and you can shift direction before spending too much time or money in a single direction.

Pause here for a minute. Think about how you've been talking about your potential customer set. What are the questions you've been getting? What is the feedback from colleagues, investors, and potential customers? If you haven't yet, take a minute to write down specifically who you believe your customer will be. At each level of granularity, also write down why you believe that to be true. This is important as we get to your second job. In "Putting W3 Together," we also use this as part of building out your sales plan.

Job 2: Disprove It

Yes, you read that correctly: disprove your own theory. Your job now is to figure out why you are right by trying to prove why you are wrong. This concept is one you'll hear from me over and over again. Of course the first thing you need to do is to validate why you believe you are right, followed by exploring why you might not be.

So what does that look like? It starts with taking that granular definition of who you believe your customer is, creating a list of 20–30 companies who fit on that list, and talking to them. Don't sell them, learn from them. We'll get into this in a lot more detail later on in the book when we talk about the difference between sales and customer development, but for now just start to think about what these conversations might look like.

The second part of that, which is job 2, is to see if you can prove yourself wrong. There are two ways to think about this. Am I wrong about the customer segment I've defined? Are they short-term customers? Are we really solving a huge pain for them? Is this really the right person in the organization to sell to? Or, is there a granular customer definition that is stronger? Will we be able to sell more, or faster, or for more money? Is there someone out there who needs us even more? Part of job 2 is to define one to two additional potential customer segments. Then try to stack-rank them. With limited time, you can probably only prioritize one group and reprioritize as you learn. This will give you the basis for proving and disproving whether your top-ranked customer set is right (and hopefully help you determine your next customer priority).

And then you have to start the process all over again.

* * *

Right now you are probably feeling a little overwhelmed. Either you are questioning how important this work really is or trying to figure out how you do this as quickly as possible. You probably don't have a lot of time or money before you need to start generating (more) revenue. That's totally normal, you should feel a bit overwhelmed. Starting a business is hard and it's a lot of responsibility. You are probably feeling the pressure of both time and money and wondering how you can do this and still hit those important milestones to raise money or slow your burn or even be profitable. Am I trying to freak you out? A little. But, more important, I'm giving you a playbook to help you avoid costly mistakes, so as you do grow you can sell more faster!

Now we've discussed who you believe your customer is, in the most granular way possible, as well as who you believe your next one or two customer sets might be. So *what* comes next!

What Is Your Customer Buying?

Identifying WHAT your customers are buying sounds obvious but it's actually much more nuanced. In fact, when you are a startup sometimes even your customers don't know what they are really buying from you. They only know what they think they want. Until you figure this out, you have no chance of building a scalable sales team.

—Kurt Rathmann, founder and CEO of ScaleFactor

What product is your customer buying? Even if you aren't sure yet who your customer is, you probably feel like you can answer the question of what you're selling with a high degree of confidence. There are two challenges with this that every startup faces. The first is, you may be wrong. Most founders get this on some level and know there will be some amount of iterating or pivoting in the pursuit of "product–market fit." What most founders and even sales leaders often overlook is that the product you are selling is often not the product the customer is buying. It's deeply important to understand that too, because it gives you the ability to identify the right buyers, craft the right pitch, and develop long-term relationships with your customers.

"Huh? What do you mean that my customers buy something different than I'm selling? That doesn't make any sense."

What You're Selling versus What the Customer Is Buying

Let me give you two examples to help paint the picture. In the first example we will look at one of my portfolio companies: LIVSN. LIVSN sells outdoor apparel for hikers and climbers. Their marketer believes that Google Adwords is a place to find customers. I will assume most people are familiar with buying Adwords on Google. In this case, Google is selling placement on a search results page specific to keywords that a Google user is searching for. Google's product is a platform to facilitate that ad buy. Is that what the marketer is buying? On the surface, yes. Dig one level deeper and what the marketer is actually buying is the attention of hikers and climbers who are in need of new apparel. Fortunately Google knows that is what the customer is buying and because of this has a stated focus (built into their product) to deliver high-quality customers for this company.

In our second example, let's look at a company that didn't initially understand the difference between what they were selling and what their customers were buying: BlackLocus.

When I joined BlackLocus, we were selling a platform that provided insight into online retailers' competitors and overlapping products. The emphasis in what we were selling was (a) the platform and (b) a snapshot in time of each customer's top competitors. What this led to for us was a misalignment with our early customers and resulted in unhappy customers and churn. However, after many customer interviews, what we learned was that (a) platform only opened the door to questions and didn't really provide anything actionable, and (b) it was more important for our customers to know how their TOP products competed online regardless of who the competitors were. While subtle, understanding these two differences helped us shape both the product and the pitch. We ultimately iterated our product to focus on our customer's products (not their competitor's) and also included suggestions (based on competitive landscape data) in the platform. These changes were instrumental in both figuring out who our customers "should be" as well as understanding how we exchanged value (product for money) with them (we'll cover this concept in more depth in Chapter 4).

To reiterate and be overly direct, there is a very important and single takeaway from these two examples – take the time to understand what your customer is actually buying (vs. what you are selling) and actually cares about. And while the difference between what you are selling and what the customer is buying is sometimes subtle, it can be the difference between building a big business or completely failing.

Knowing Your What

So how do we figure out the *what?* It starts with another series of questions that you pose to real prospects and customers. Here is an example of some of those questions (we'll get more in-depth on this topic in the "Putting W3 Together" section). *What* are they buying? What product/feature is the customer buying? What problem are you solving for that buyer? How will they buy your product? How will they pay for your product?

Let's start at the beginning—meaning the day you were sitting at the coffee shop and had that aha moment that it was time for you to start a company and you had just the right idea. This was the moment when you decided to leave the security of your current life and jump in, feet first, to build a huge company.

This may sound corny but close your eyes and take 20 seconds to try and remember the exact feelings you had that day. Remember the problem you identified and remember how excited you were when you realized you were uniquely equipped to solve that problem and build the next unicorn. Now write down the product you want to sell followed by a list of three to five things you believe your product solves for your customer. Next look at each one of those items and write down one to three questions for each that you can pose to potential customers from your *who* list.

However, before you go do that, try to answer them yourself. Write down your answers so you can refer back to them and see where you were right or wrong. There are two reasons to do this: first, it will provide a history for you of how your product and thinking is shaped and evolves based on what your customer is actually buying (and *why,* which we'll get to in the next section). And second, if you pay close attention, you can also learn about the way in which your customer set does business by listening to both the answers and the language that your customers use. This data will become important further on when we dig into building your sales process, which is why I want you to record it.

If you are like me, you may have started this work as you were reading this section; that's great, but don't worry if you didn't, we'll get deeper into it in the exercises in the "Putting W3 Together" section. More important to take away from this section is an understanding and belief that you need to understand what your customer is actually buying from you in order for you to build the correct product. Now that you understand the difference between *what* you are selling and *what* your customer is buying, we can move on to the *why.*

Why Is Your Customer Buying It?

If I asked you that question, you'd likely give me either your problem statement or mission statement. For most founders, *why* their customer is buying their product is the entire reason they are building their company. But there are actually three questions that need to be answered here:

1. Why you believe they will buy your product
2. Why they say they (may) buy your product
3. Why they really buy your product

Why *You Believe They Will Buy Your Product*

This is the entire reason you exist, to solve a problem or gap for your end user. Likely this is the problem statement in your sales and investor deck. This is also what you answer when people ask you what your company does. Great! This is exactly where you should start. *Why* you believe your customer will buy your product is exactly the flag in the ground you need to get started; just keep in mind that it is simply a starting point and without understanding the other *why*s, it's nearly impossible to build a really big and scaled business.

In order to help you understand the next two whys, we're going to start with an example. At Business.com, we believed our customers bought our product to reach more of their target customers: small and medium-sized businesses (SMBs). This was our core message and how we talked about the value of Business.com for our customers, and while on the surface we were right, there was more motivation that our customers needed before they would actually spend money with us. This is where the next two *why*s come into play.

Why *Prospective Customers Say They (May) Buy Your Product*

Think about this as the actual problem you are solving for your customer on the business level. When this aligns perfectly with your first *why*, you are in a great place, but they actually don't need to be perfectly aligned as long as you understand this second *why* and can address it. Remember in the case of Business.com, we believed our customers bought our product to reach more of their target customers. While this is true, that meant something different to each of our customers. For some, that meant actually driving direct sales (i.e. the expectation was that when a user left Business.com and went to a website a transaction would take place). Those customers measured us on direct transactions, also known as sales of their product.

Other customers of ours bought Business.com because they were buying leads (or prospective customers for their business). And while ultimately they were looking to drive more sales, their expectation wasn't that a transaction would take place immediately. Instead they would have their own system to nurture leads that came from Business.com and their own process to eventually turn some quantity of leads into sales.

And we even had a third kind of buyer who was buying Business .com for measured awareness. They didn't expect or track transactions from Business.com, but they did track the number of people who were exposed to their company from Business.com.

For us, at Business.com, it was important to understand the business reason why each buyer was buying our product because it gave us insight into their ability to reach their goals and be successful in buying our product, which translated into our ability to acquire long-term happy customers. Over time, what we learned was that the middle group, companies looking to build a lead/nurture list, was the most successful group on Business.com. There is an entirely different book that can likely be written on this topic, but we classified our product and customers by thinking about the stage that their customer is in when they came to Business.com. Those stages are *learn, find,* and *buy.* The *learn* stage meant that someone was on Business.com doing initial research on a product and trying to collect information so they would be able to make an informed decision down the road. We learned early on that "learning" was not our main role. That doesn't mean that millions of users didn't come to Business.com monthly to learn about a product they may buy in the future; in fact, they did. And we had a very specific user experience designed for them. However, our experience showed that when *our* customer was looking to primarily drive awareness they, for several different reasons, were not our best customers and often had higher churn.

"Buy" is the first *why* I listed above, which means there was an expectation of a transaction once a user left Business.com and went to our customer's website. While we were able to drive some level of transactions, what we learned was that for B2B sales (and specially SMB sales), it was very rare for a user to make many purchases off any website and often they wanted to buy from a person (either because of product type or the cost of the merchandise). And while there were some products (i.e. toner cartridges) for which we were able to drive high volumes of transactions, *buy* wasn't really our sweet spot either.

That brings us to the middle of the funnel: *find*. This is the spot between a user doing research and actually making a purchase where they are trying to find a specific vendor (or vendors) to buy from. This is where Business.com really shined for our customers. And once we understood this, we were much better positioned to find and acquire high-value customers. Understanding this *why* gave us the ability to narrow our core target base by asking a simple question in the sales process around what our prospects hoped to achieve by working with us. We would tease out of the conversation whether their expectation was learn, find, or buy and emphasize selling to customers who fell into the "find" category. This understanding also gave us the ability to do things within our product to help drive more qualified leads to our customers. ("Qualified leads" means a buyer who actually has intent to make a purchase.) We were able to shape the product with layout, product descriptions, and a user experience that made it clear to our user what they were supposed to do and how to do it. Likewise having this understanding with our customers gave us a clear pathway to understanding how they would measure success using Business.com, which in turn lets us become their partner in achieving that success.

I realize there is a lot to absorb in the last few paragraphs, so let's pause and I'll state it in a different way. Our customers were focused on the *find*-stage. If we were focused on providing *learning*-stage users to them, then we would likely be focused on *quantity* rather than on *quality* of users. We would have designed our product to focus on attracting as many people to their site as possible, with little regard for whether they would ever buy. Likewise, if we were focused on the *buying*-stage users, we might have gotten very good at finding users to transact on our customers websites, but we would not have been able to work with any business that had a more complex or higher value product. By focusing on *find*, we were able to strike the perfect balance between delivering quantity while being held to a quality standard. And for this reason, when we had the right customer type, we had very low churn. At the time I left Business.com, we had below 1% customer churn and net positive revenue churn.

Why *They Really Buy Your Product*

This brings us to the last *why*—why your customer *really* buys your product. This is often the hardest one to figure out, but often the one that will actually drive the close of your sales. This has to do with your actual buyer. Let's step back and recap on the first two *why*s first. Our first *why* is your belief in the problem *you* believe you are solving for your potential customer. In the case of Business.com, that was to sell more of their products or services and increase their revenue. Our second *why* is why they say they (may) buy your product. This is the business reason. In the case of Business com, it was because our customers were looking at our users as people who could either learn, find, or buy their products through Business.com. Conventional wisdom might say that you have all the information you need but, as discussed earlier, there is one more crucial *why* to be answered: *why* they really buy your product. This *why* has to do with the motivation of your buyer.

Your buyer could be motivated for any number of reasons, from their boss telling them they had to buy your product or to help them save time or because they are driving toward a specific metric as part of their job. When you understand this *why*, you have unlocked the final piece in helping secure a sale and a happy customer, because along with focusing on the success of their business you can also help focus on their personal success. I get more into that at the end of the "Why" section, but for now let's dig deeper into understanding why your customer really buys your product.

Think about your own job for a minute. Whether you are a founder/CEO of an early stage company, head of sales, or fill some other role in your company, think about your own buying habits. To illustrate my point, let's imagine that I'm selling Business.com as a service to an established company that sells credit card processors. For this example, let's also assume that this marketer is good at their job, highly regarded within their company, and hitting all their goals. Before buying our product, there is no way for them to tell how we might affect their goal attainment, and therefore no real motivation for them to go out on a limb to buy from us (too). In this scenario, picture that we have nailed the first two *whys* perfectly, yet we really do not know what the third *why* is yet, why our customer would actually buy from us.

It's at this point that we need to dig deeper to understand our buyer's personal motivation to become a customer. Can we save them time? Money? Can we help them meet or exceed their goals? Can we help them satisfy their boss? Are you starting to see why this *why* is so important? We are all very busy and in order to cross the final threshold into making a sale, it's imperative that we understand the underlying motivation of our buyer. And there is no substitute here for just asking the question. Personally I like to be very direct about it and will say something like, "we've agreed that Business.com can bring you more qualified leads, but how does this help you in your job? Does it make things easier or harder and let's talk about it." This simple line of questioning opens up an entirely new conversation around personal motivation to become a customer and it gives you, the seller, the ability to set up this customer to be successful.

Measuring Your—and Your Customer's—Why

The final thing I want to say about *why* is that, although knowing about it is crucial, knowing how to *measure* it is imperative.

Arguably the concepts of measuring and metrics deserve their own section in this book, but I'm intentionally introducing the topic now to alert you to its importance. Whatever it is that we're talking about in W3 or *Sell More Faster* or your business, understanding what should be measured, how to measure it, and how that affects our ability to build a big business will always be an underlying factor. And that is the same for all of our (potential) customers. We'll directly (and indirectly) get into measuring *who* and *what* throughout the book as we talk about building prospect lists and iterating the product. But we're going to talk about measuring *why* here. Why, you ask? Because if we do not deeply understand how our prospective customer will measure their success, then we have no real way to know *if* our product is working, *what* about it is working, or *why* it's working. We'll also have no way to predict how we should evolve our product or service, pitch it, or even *who* our customers should be. And, worst of all, we'll have no way to predict churn or why we are losing customers.

Getting to the core of how our customers measure *why* is fundamental to acquiring high value, low-churn customers, and building a big business. Let's take a look, using the same example from above, with the marketer who sells credit card processors. For this example, we'll assume that we've checked the first two *why* boxes and know that this is a great prospective customer. We have a conversation with our buyer and we learn two things. The first is that our buyer will be measuring our success by using Google Analytics and will have an expectation of a 10% close rate within 60 days with an average customer value of $200. The second thing we learn is that our buyer's supervisor hasn't typically believed that search marketing, outside of Google, was very effective, even though our buyer believes they are missing a lot of opportunity. We now understand that our buyer, while maybe a believer, has a heightened motivation around quality and likely less room for error because she will have to put her neck out in order to test with something other than Google, but also that if we're able to help drive new and incremental sales, then we will help our buyer build credibility internally, which will help her career. Because our buyer has been clear both about the metrics she is shooting for and her own motivations, we are able to work with her to reach those goals.

In contrast, and as a way to help understand the importance of understanding how your customer will measure and be measured for success, take the same buyer with the same method of measuring business success (10%/60 days/$200 average order), but in this case our buyer is considered the expert by their supervisor and our buyer has no external motivation to drive additional net new sales (meaning that she is hitting her expressed goals from her supervisor with no additional incentive to go beyond these goals). This happens a lot and is often the biggest reason why sales don't close. Assuming that you still have the first two *whys* nailed, you have to dig deeper to see what might motivate this buyer. It could be that something in the product helps them save time or money. Or it could be that your product doesn't match with this buyer's personal *why*. That doesn't mean this company can't be a customer but it does likely mean that you do not have the right buyer within that company. You may need to go to their supervisor because their motivations are more aligned or you may need to find a completely new buyer within the organization.

Okay, we're going to pause for a second. I just gave you a ton of information on *why*. I know it's a lot to process at once. That's okay; a lot of this probably makes perfect sense already and some of it you may just need to experience firsthand. In any case, I'm going to boil down *why* here for you, which is to say that understanding *why* a prospect becomes a customer, while complex, is the final but most important part of W3. It's the thing that binds the *who* and the *what* together and gives you the ability to define your ICP (ideal customer profile, remember that) and the confidence to articulate it to staff, investors, and customers.

Putting W3 Together

For me, being able to define W3 is literally the basis for every conversation with every founder I work with because, while we are discussing it here in terms of selling more faster, W3 touches upon so much more. As discussed earlier, understanding your W3 helps shape your product, pitch, marketing, the technology you build, and every aspect of your business. It also gives you the ability to articulate your business to your staff in a way that will connect and align the roles they fulfill in your company. Likewise, investors will be able to paint a clearer picture of what they are investing in and how your business will potentially grow (and, more important, the process you will use to figure out how to build a big business). Furthermore, it will make it clear to your customers why you exist, making it easier to align with their needs and work with them for the long term.

In order to help you on your journey, most sections in this book end with an exercise so that you have a structured framework and put pen to paper. After each exercise there will be an example with the answers filled in, so that you can refer to them as you go along. Don't hesitate to flip back and forth to my example; just keep in mind that the answers from the example are specific to that business and may not directly apply to yours. The other thing to keep in mind here is that it's okay to guess when you don't know—guessing will be your hypothesis of what you currently believe. Take special care to mark what you know as fact versus what matches your hypothesis, so that you can test your beliefs in the quest to improve your W3.

Bringing W3 Together

Who Are You Selling To?

Write down a description of *who* your ideal customer is:

- Define their profile. (This is the granular attributes of who you think your customer is. An example could be by industry, company size, job title, or all of these.)
- Define how you segment. (This is how you develop your customer profile and create different segments to sell to, so that you can prioritize where you spend time selling.)
- Define how you will prioritize each segment.
- Who do you think is the target buyer at each customer? (This is the actual person/job title in a company.)
- Write down *why* you think the target you just described is your target customer:
  - Define what your target customer currently does without having your product.
  - Define how your product makes your customer grow revenue and improve margin, and how it makes their job easier compared to their current process.
  - Define how your product will affect those whom your customer works with (departmental dependencies).

What Are They Buying?

- Write down the product you are selling.
- Write down the product they are buying.
- If there is a difference between what you are selling and what they are buying, write it down.

Why Are They Buying?

- Write down *why* you believe the customer will buy your product.
- Write down *why* the customer actually buys your product.
- If there is a difference between why you believe they will buy and why they actually buy, write it down.
- Write down your theory on the tangible value you provide (in $ if possible) and justify it:
  - How will your customer measure that value?
  - How will your customer be measured on that value?
  - How will you measure that value (for you and your customer)?

Once you have a strawman for the above, Chapter 2 walks you through how to take your entire hypothesis and begin proving it, using the customer development process. The following is an example using Business.com as a reference for your own answers.

W3: Business.com Example

Business.com was a B2B search engine and directory. We sold cost-per-click (CPC) ad placements and connected businesses looking to buy products and suppliers to fill their needs.

Who Are You Selling To?

Write down who you think your customers is: At Business.com, we determined that our ideal customer was the adwords/search buyer at companies that were trying to sell their products or services to small and medium-sized businesses (SMBs). We chose the buyer because this was when the concept of ad words was still somewhat new and novel—we didn't want to spend time educating prospects; instead we wanted to work with people who already saw the value in search advertising. We chose the buyer's target (SMBs) because we concluded (and later proved) that the opportunity breadth for SMBs was exponentially greater than enterprise targets (fewer of them, they buy less often, and they are slower to make decisions).

Define their profile: Digital marketers, whose products or services corresponded with the pages on Business.com with heavy search and directory traffic (i.e. available inventory). Typically our buyer was under 35, highly analytical and reported to a director or VP. Their title was usually manager or director of search advertising. If a company did not have a dedicated search buyer, we would deprioritize them, because it meant that either senior leadership didn't yet understand the power and value of search advertising *or* the search buyer wasn't analytical enough to understand conversion metrics.

Define how you segment: Once we had an ideal customer profile, we used several tools including azoogle, our own search data, Google, and publicly available lists of digital advertisers to create a list of over 40,000 potential customers (website, buyer name, proxy for digital spend, and search terms typically purchased), and segmented first by spend on Google and second by number of keywords purchased on Google. Next we looked at the buyer's title (see earlier) and pulled out anyone who didn't match our ideal customer profile.

Define how you will prioritize each segment: The cross-reference mentioned above created a stack-ranked priority list of highest revenue opportunity on Business.com. This means that we created a way to rank all of the prospects and then we prioritized them from "most important" to "least important." We (three directors, two managers, and me) then split up the top 10,000 companies (roughly 1,500 each) and reviewed each website for contact information and to find duplicates. This gave us our final prospect list, which we handed to our sales team.

Who do you think is the target buyer at each customer?: This is answered above.

Write down why you think they are your target customer: We believed this was our target customer because they already showed an appetite for highly targeted digital direct marketing as part of their customer acquisition strategy *and* we believed we were able to deliver highly targeted and high-quality prospects looking for a product or service they offered.

Define what they currently do without having your product: At Business.com this was a tough question. We had to turn a negative into a positive, meaning that in some respects they already had our product, thanks to Google. In many cases it was hard for our prospects to comprehend why they would need us, too. This forced us to focus on the quality of the traffic we sent their way and also to create a high-touch client service relationship.

We knew we couldn't (and didn't want to) replace Google, so instead we focused on quality over quantity. Because of this, we had virtually no customer attrition. Ultimately what we had to prove (and did) was that Google provided quantity (often at a lower price), but we provided quality they couldn't live without, to meet their sales goals.

Define how your product makes your customer grow revenue and improve margins and/or how it makes their job easier compared to their current process. In the case of Business.com, our value proposition was to help our customers grow revenue directly because we were a channel for them to acquire customers. That said, if we were not able to do that profitably, or if our product was too hard to use, we would not have been successful at selling or retaining our customers because they had alternatives.

Business.com provided high-quality leads to our customers as well as the tools to spend the right amount of money to acquire those customers at their target margins.

Define how your product will affect the people whom your customer works with (departmental dependencies): This is a key and often overlooked part of the sales process. Even if you have the right buyer, who has the ability to approve the sale, sometimes there are other people or departments involved with the implementation. This can cause the implementation to be slow, suboptimized, or even killed. You need to know this, and you need to ask this any time you are not completely sure of the answer.

At Business.com, this was key to how we prioritized whom we sold to. When a customer needed their tech department to implement tracking tags (vs. doing it themselves) we knew the go-live date would often be delayed (and sometimes by a lot). We would always ask this question and then work to get ahead of it, both in terms of implementation (developing a plan that included the appropriate technical person) and by forecasting the close date of those deals. Ultimately we wouldn't close a deal until we had technical buy-in and commitment on an implementation date.

What Are They Buying?

Write down the product you are selling: At Business.com we sold cost-per-click (CPC) advertising.

Write down the product they are buying: At Business.com our customers were buying (high-quality) leads and customers (depending on their landing pages).

If there is a difference between what you are selling and what they are buying, write it down: In our case there was a difference, and it was important to understand. We sold ad space and our customers were buying leads. In theory, they didn't care what our product looked like, as long as the "thing" we delivered to them was leads (ideally high-quality leads).

Here is an example: if we focused on what we sold, then our pitch and product efforts would be around maximizing ad inventory on our site and quantity of leads sent their way (regardless of quality). Because we understood what our customers were buying, we focused on optimizing and delivering quality leads to their website.

Why Are They Buying?

Write down why you believe the customer will buy your product: At Business.com, we believed the customer bought our product to sell more of their products or services and increase their revenue.

Write down why the customer actually buys your product: In most cases, our customer was a mid-level employee. The reason our customer bought our product was to hit the goals their supervisor gave them so that they would be perceived as doing a good job.

If there is a difference between why you believe they will buy and why they actually buy, write it down: The company you're selling to is trying to drive sales. Often however, the actual customer was trying to hit their goals. Take a minute to think about the different motivations. The company wants revenue. The employee wants to do good work and keep their job; they may or may not always care about the bigger picture. This is important to know prior to the sale, so you can understand how to work with your customer so that the employee hits their goals, the company hits their goals—and we hit ours.

Write down your theory on the tangible value you provide (in dollars if possible) and justify it: At Business.com, we provided direct customer and revenue increases for our customers.

How will your customer measure that value?: At Business.com, our customer measured the value we provided by looking at their sales numbers and cost per customer, and the more savvy customers also looked at lifetime value of our customers (vs. other sources).

How will your customer be measured on that value: Our customer was measured on their ability to buy leads or customers by quantity and with an expectation of cost per customer within given bounds. In other words, there was a cap on what they could spend with us and still acquire a profitable customer.

How will you measure that value (for you and your customer)?: This is hard; accept this challenge in advance. It's also critical if you want your customer base to be high value and long lasting.

It starts with really candid and transparent conversations up-front, before a sale is made. It's imperative that you ask your customer how they will measure success and what success looks like for them. And then don't just take it on face value, ask them why (and why again). Get to the root. Make sure they have the tools, intelligence, and ability to know and measure the results.

Make this conversation part of the sales process, and use it as a way to continually check in to make sure goals are being hit (and not being shifted without your knowledge, leaving you with no way to help your customer succeed). At Business.com we realized that while most of our customers used Google Analytics well to measure their Google campaigns, they did not have the tools to measure ours. This helped guide our product development efforts: we both built a way to add our campaigns into their Google Analytics and also developed our own analytics tool (so we could also track metrics). We provided exceptional customer service by always being in step with—if not a step ahead of—how our customers were doing.

Chapter 2

Finding Your First Customers

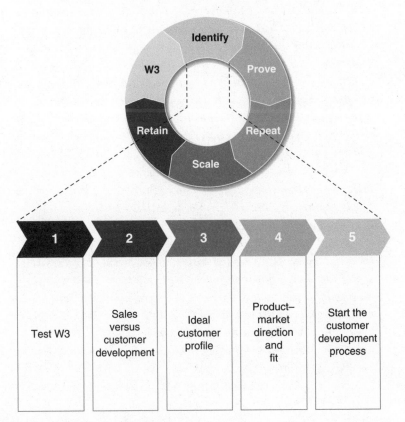

Figure 2.1 Find Your First Customers

Over 20 years of taking new technology to market and working across startups, like Bazaarvoice and Convey, focused on acquiring customers across many different markets, the simple axiom of "know thy customer" rings truer to me now more than ever.

I have been on both sides of this, having a lot of early customer acquisition success with early adopters and then scaling to the next wave of customers too early. Without doing the really hard, roll your sleeves up, work of asking the fundamental questions about the customer's struggle, why it matters and what business pain it is attached to, it is nearly impossible to calculate meaningful ROI that they are willing to pay for.

I believe what drives us to want to move fast and to shortcut this critical process is #1 the fear that our window of opportunity to be first will collapse and competitors will move in quickly, and #2 that somehow simplifying the proposition too much and narrowing too far will diminish the value of the offering.

Real immersion in your customer's struggle is the key. At this vital step in the journey your early adopters are willing to engage in helping you to articulate and clearly define a pain, challenge, or opportunity (PCO) that is not widely known or recognized. They believe that solving the problem will translate to out-sized results and will make them look like a superstar innovator and performer to their company and peers.

You can't move into selling in a repeatable, at scale way until this PCO has been fleshed out, well documented and publicized in a way that the broader, early majority market can begin to raise their hand and identify with it.

A real risk here is that effective early stage salespeople can sell past these shortcuts and at least for some period of time show strong customer acquisition among early adopters. The result is the painful discovery two years into the journey that you have hit a scaling wall because you haven't taken the time to do that hard work to truly understand the business you're in. Fixing it at that point can be extremely daunting if it's even possible because you are effectively starting over.

—Chris Richter, VP of revenue at Convey

The W3 Framework Is Worthless … Until You Test It!

In Chapter 1 we used the W3 framework to identify the *who, what,* and *why*: that is, *who* do we believe our customer is, *what* are they buying from us, and *why* does our product meet their needs. We do this on the quest to achieve what every company is ultimately looking for, product–market fit. If you aren't familiar with this concept, then I implore you to get very familiar with it, because without it you don't have a sustainable company. Product–market fit is the degree to which a product satisfies a strong market demand. In other words, if your product doesn't fit your market, you will have no demand and therefore no business. We cover this in greater detail further on in this chapter.

In this chapter we will take the W3 work from the Chapter 1 test and prove it, in the real world, through the customer development process, with the goal of identifying our ICP (ideal customer profile) and *early signs* of product–market fit (which I define as product–market direction; Figure 2.1). Going out and testing this work, collecting data on why you are right (or not) is imperative before you attempt to scale your sales organization.

There is a very common error I see here, especially among first-time founders, which is that once they feel like they can describe even partial aspects of W3, they think they are ready to start hiring several salespeople and start scaling revenue. This is actually where you need to pause and go try to prove why your theory on your W3 is correct. While this may, on the surface, feel like slowing down the train, there are a few reasons this is crucial to actually selling more faster, starting with the fact that it reduces the chance that you are wrong *after* you've hired a bunch of people and are far down a particular customer path. It also gives you data that will inform the sales process (we discuss this more in Chapter 3) and finally, it'll provide more data (and confidence) to investors, which should lead to greater funding and ability to scale faster.

Before we get into the work part of this chapter, I'd like to share one personal example to help set context for why the customer development process is so important.

The Wrong W3

I joined BlackLocus in early 2012 as head of sales. BlackLocus sold competitive pricing and assortment analytics to online retailers. What this meant was that we could tell a retailer (1) who their competitors were, (2) how their products were priced relative to their competitors, (3) what products they sold that their competitors did not sell, and (4) what products they did not sell that their competitors did sell. In theory, anyone with an online retail presence could use our product. It didn't really matter if you were selling dog beds, hammers, shoes, or vitamins. If the product had a decent description, we'd be able to identify our customers' competitors anywhere on the web.

When I joined the company they had already hired a seasoned and good, later-stage, salesperson (we'll call him John). John had closed roughly 15 customers when I joined. As my first task, I tried to determine our W3. After speaking with John, some customers, our CEO, and our head of product, it was still unclear to me *who* our ideal customer was, *what* the customer was buying, or *why* they needed our product.

Up to that point, John believed he should be able to sell to anyone with an online retail presence because the value proposition (being able to tell our customers how their products were priced relative to their competitors) was relatively similar and by itself should persist. While John did a good job closing several early customers, BlackLocus was caught in a vicious cycle of (many) unhappy customers who were churning as fast as John was acquiring new ones.

The cycle was that John would spend time and resources selling a customer and getting them to believe our ability, only to result in that customer leaving a few months later. Our revenue wasn't shrinking or growing, it was simply not moving, because John was replacing customers at the same rate we were losing them. We didn't have a clear picture of our *who*, we didn't really understand *what* are customers were buying (only what we were selling), and therefore no idea *why* customers were buying. The customer profiles were all over the map, making it impossible to triangulate on *what or why* they were buying (or not buying).

Defining BlackLocus's W3

When I joined, I didn't have a strong opinion of our W3. I understood what we were selling, but I wasn't really sure *what* our customers were buying and therefore had no idea *why* they bought (or how they would measure success). I spent the first three months questioning everything and talking to both existing and potential customers of all sizes, industries, experience level, location, and so on. I even went outside the retail world simply to try and disprove our theory about our e-commerce focus. You can see, at the end of this chapter, examples of the types of things you can question (by which I mean *everything*).

In that three months I was able to narrow down our W3 and define it clearly as "large retailers with over $50 million in revenue who had a strong online presence." Taking it further, I learned that our customers should be retailers whose products were hard goods and often commodity items like drills, hammers, electronics, and so on. This could range from home improvement chains to big electronics chains, as well as bigger retailers who sold branded items where a SKU number was used across all retailers. The reason we learned this was because commodity items and typically hard goods are clearly defined and easy to identify, making the competitor sets easier to identify. Additionally, they typically have tighter margins for our customers, which makes them higher priority. These aspects combined made our impact on their businesses bigger and easier to measure.

Finally, I learned that if the company didn't have a role whose job was specifically focused on pricing analytics, then the likelihood of a successful sale or implementation became dramatically decreased.

There are two primary reasons why this became an important characteristic. First, when a company centralized their pricing efforts, it demonstrated that the company put a high value on optimizing price and margins, and second, by centralizing their pricing efforts I now had one main buyer versus a decentralized model where there would be many people that we would need to convince that we could do an aspect of their job faster and with more accuracy. The fact that I had fewer people to sell to and the importance the organization put on the effort could decrease the time to close by six months or more! Let me describe to you the difference.

Centralized pricing efforts: When a company centralized their pricing efforts, it meant a few things. First and foremost, there was one person (or department) responsible for all pricing decisions. This was important for us because it meant fewer people whom we had to convince that BlackLocus would save them time and make them more money. It also meant that they likely used data, in some form, to make pricing decisions. Sometimes this would be a complex algorithm around self-identified products and competitors, and sometimes it was as simple as a person managing a spreadsheet. In any case, it demonstrated to us that the company believed data (not intuition) was better for driving pricing decisions. Finally, and maybe most important, our observation was that companies who had a centralized pricing function were typically more tech-forward in general and looking for scale efficiency—which was at the core of what our product promised to deliver.

Decentralized pricing efforts: When a company had a decentralized pricing strategy it usually meant that the buyers or merchandising team would make pricing decisions individually for the product lines they were responsible for. In a big retailer there could be dozens or even hundreds of buyers. Right off the bat, this made the idea of selling a much bigger challenge. Can you imagine if you had to get buy-in from 50 or more people to sell one single customer? Additionally, while some of the people making pricing decisions at these retailers did use some form of technology (even if just to track pricing changes with their products), our observation was that these retailers typically thought that some of their competitive advantage was the individual buyer's or merchandiser's expertise. Right or wrong, inherently in that line of thinking was a rejection that any company (BlackLocus or any of our competitors) would ever do their job better than them. The uphill battle of trying to convince dozens or more people whose initial reaction was that we could not do their job better seemed silly, and therefore we tried to stay away from those retailers.

Next I learned what our customers wanted and were buying, which was "competitive insights" for their highest valued/velocity items. This was different than what we were selling (pricing analytics for their entire catalogue) and while the product was mostly the same it provided how we should be pitching BlackLocus.

Next, understanding the *who* and *what* lead me to the *why*, which was at a macro level almost always the same (to price competitively against competitors), but almost always varied from a single competitor, a series of competitors, or in some cases just Amazon.

Measuring Value with an ROI Calculator

Understanding the *why* also gave me the ability to develop a system to measure value transfer, so that our customers (and we) would understand the direct monetary impact to their business. This system was a one-two punch. First was the development of our ROI calculator (Figure 2.2). The ROI calculator took into account both the potential revenue increases to their business as well as margin increases and operation efficiencies resulting from using BlackLocus.

The calculator was a series of formulas where the company's variables (number of products, pricing changes, increase in sales, and margin contribution) could all be tinkered with, giving our customer a clear idea of how their business could be affected if they worked with us and what the return on investment (ROI) would be to them.

The second part of the one-two punch was that we made the ROI calculator a part of the sales process. Once we identified a need with a prospective customer (and the customer acknowledged there could be a fit), the next step would be to share the calculator and work with our prospective customer in filling in all the variables. We already had confidence in our product's ability to work, and the calculator would let us all get on the same page about how well it would work. Once the prospective customer saw how BlackLocus would impact their business, we knew the sale was inevitable.

Now, there were a handful of cases where the ROI calculator showed minimal or no real impact to a retailer. In these cases, this was also a huge win because we knew then that this wasn't a good long-term customer, so we'd walk away. While this didn't

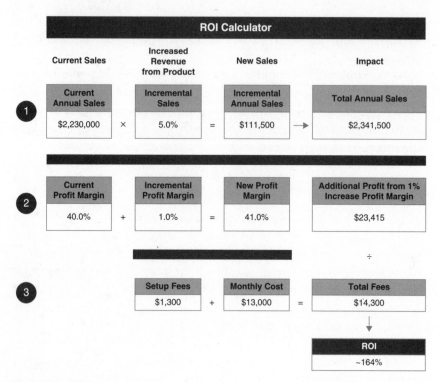

Figure 2.2   ROI Calculator
Source: Courtesy of Austin Dressen.

happen very often, cases where it did happen usually meant that the customer didn't sell a lot of products and the products they did sell had such a small margin that there simply wasn't enough volume of data to have a meaningful impact.

Knowing this was also great because we wouldn't waste any additional time or resources on a customer who wasn't a good fit for our business. Not all revenue is good revenue, and knowing when to walk away from a sale is equally as important as knowing when not to.

At the point when we figured this out, our revenue was roughly $10,000 in monthly recurring revenue (MRR). Within six months our revenue jumped to over $120,000 in MRR because we knew exactly who to sell to, what they were buying, and how to articulate the value to their business. In our case, we nailed the ICP so quickly and directly that in less than a year after identifying our

ICP we sold the company to Home Depot for over $50 million on less than $1.5 million in annual revenue.

Lessons Learned

A few things I want to point out specific to going through a customer development cycle:

1. **Three months felt long.** The company's CEO and board were initially concerned about halting growth. They were worried that taking the time to step back and prove (or in this case disprove) the initial theory on their W3 would slow down revenue plans. As I hope this story points out, taking the time to define and prove our W3 actually did help us to *sell more faster.*

2. **Three months was short,** actually, and we listened well. What I mean here is that, had we instead kept with the initial plan, while we would have potentially increased revenue, we would have stayed in that vicious cycle of sell-churn-sell-churn. It's hard to say how long the customer development process will take—it could be three months or it could be much longer, though it's rarely much shorter, simply because you need time to collect enough data to prove/disprove your theory. By listening well, I mean that we took the time to ask lots of question, collect data from our targets, and then test our theories to confirm we understood what our customers were saying.

3. Had we not gone through this process, we would have continued to sell small and medium-sized businesses (SMBs) and had high churn, low revenue, and no exit.

* * *

A common pitfall here, especially with early sales, is that you get a few prospects to say "yes" and pay you. You may close 5, 10, or more customers (depending on the potential size of your ICP pool) so you start ramping sales. This is the time to stop and question everything. Confirmation bias, which is defined as the tendency to search for answers that confirm our hypothesis, can be one of the most dangerous things for a sales team—your job at this point is to disprove that your ICP theory is correct! Once you start seeing some real traction, it's time to go back to your theory and ask yourself why you might be wrong, to see if you can disprove it and/or find limitations.

If you can't disprove your theory, then you have directional indicators of product–market fit and are ready to test scaling your sales team. If you are a business-to-customer (B2C) company, the same principles apply. You may get really good at bringing people to your site or downloading your app, but then usage falls or the value your users find in your product is much different than you believed it would be. B2C is only more complicated in that you'll need to spend more time understanding in-depth dynamics of usage and repeat-usage to truly nail your ideal customer profile (ICP).

All too often founders reject this idea. They believe that by limiting their ICP early on or questioning early positive signals, they will limit their full potential and/or ability to scale quickly. I've personally been here dozens of times, both directly and indirectly through my personal investments, and my experience says the opposite, which is that maniacally focusing on identifying and proving your ICP is crucial in scaling long-term customers and building a sustainable business.

Sales versus Customer Development

> *When we first entered Techstars we thought we had a strong idea of our ICP, but what we learned was that it was too broad. We took a small step back and ran a customer development process, which lead to us clearly proving our ICP which has resulted in skyrocketing sales.*
>
> —Kurt Rathmann, founder and CEO of ScaleFactor

So what does all this have to do with the difference between *sales* and *customer development?* The next step in building a highly scalable sales organization is to prove (with data) your W3 theory through the customer development process. To do this, it's first important to understand the difference between sales and customer development. This is an important distinction and until you've gone through at least one full customer development cycle (and likely more) to largely prove your theory, you are not ready to start selling at scale.

Let me say that again, slightly differently to drive home the point—*stop selling!* You aren't ready. First, by using the customer development process, prove why you are correct in your theory of your W3.

Here is how we will define the two:

Sales: We all know what sales is—it's exchanging money for goods or services. The kid with the lemonade stand and the founder with the multimillion-dollar medical device are doing the same thing: trying to convince you to pull out your wallet and exchange your money for their product. And *Webster's* dictionary defines "sales" as the exchange of goods or services for an amount of money or its equivalent.

Customer development is not a well-known term and there are a lot of definitions of what "customer development" means. The definition I like best is by Steve Blank, attributed with creating the customer development concept, the practice of gaining customer insights to generate, test, and optimize ideas for products and services through interviews and structured experiments.

I would add to Steve's definition one element that I believe is crucial, which is getting people to exchange real value (and ideally pay) for early versions of your product (even if your product is still your minimum viable product [MVP]). Yes, you read that correctly, even if your product is in its most basic and minimum form, simply hearing someone say they would want it is not enough proof for you to claim product–market fit. Your customers, even your earliest customers, need to put their money where their mouth is. This means that before you let them use your product and become a customer, they need to pay you something for it. Ideally that is money, but at minimum there should be some sort of ongoing time commitment from the customer that demonstrates both their desire for continued use of your product and in the best cases their willingness to help you improve the product they are using. The reason this is critical is because it's really easy for anyone to offer up ideas (even great ones) but until someone is willing to exchange value (money, time, or information) there is no proof they or anyone else will.

Your company is not ready to go from customer development into sales until you clearly know your W3 and it's been largely proven through the customer development process with data to back it up. You must have strong conviction with proof of *who* your customer is (also known as ICP), *what* they are buying, and *why* they are buying it. Additionally, you (and your customers) should have a well-defined and repeatable understanding and way to measure the value transfer.

In its simplest form, this "value transfer" can be explained as both you and your customer feeling like the trade between your product and the money they pay you to use it is reasonable. Your customer ideally has a way to measure the value they receive from your product relative to what they are paying you (and it should be a positive ROI for them). Likewise, you believe that the money you are receiving from them is both fair and, more important, covers the expense of running your business, ideally with healthy margins.

I do want to make a very important note here, which is that early on, especially when you are in customer development mode, it's likely that you are underpriced and that your customer is getting greater value from your product than what you are charging them for. My personal philosophy here is that is normal and expected—and that you won't find true price elasticity until your business is much more mature. If you try optimizing for (a higher) price too early on, you'll run the risk of getting false negatives and hearing no from real potential customers. I believe it's better to undercharge early customers so that (i) you know they are willing to pay something ongoing and (ii) lower the barrier for your early customers who say yes. Assuming your product delivers high value, finding the right balance for price can be tackled later. We will cover this in greater depth in Chapter 4.

Once you have this proof, you are ready to build and scale your sales team. Until then you are in customer development mode.

For me, pivoting is justified in two situations: (1) lack of Value-Market-Fit, where what you are pitching (value) does not resonate (regardless of if the product is quite to the point of sustaining true customer "happiness"). Think of Value-Market-Fit as being able to walk in and close 9/10 customers. (2) If you found this fit, but the opportunity size (*Total Addressable Market*), is not large enough to support the size of business you are trying to create.

When we entered Techstars we were focused on chasing the metrics of revenue and growth after some early traction and hiring a few salespeople, without paying attention to whether we had achieved VMF. This led to churn, unsustainable customer growth, and issues with sales funnel metrics.

When we finally stepped back and honed in on finding the core value in our offering, we were able to refocus and find repeatable success with our pitch to our target personas. Knowing that while our product might not be there yet, we knew the value we were building was sustainable gave us a foundation to build from. As founder, I had to be the one to figure this out; I hired sales too early and delayed this realization. The key was being honest with ourselves and looking deeply at whether the signals we were tracking and the traction we were getting was actually an indicator of a market fit or just early revenue.

—Noah Spirakus, CEO and founder, Prospectify

Another reason this distinction is important is around hiring. The profile of someone who does sales versus someone who does customer development is pretty different. We'll spend more time on hiring in Chapter 5, but here are a couple of quick differences between the two.

Salespeople
- Need and sell much more when they have a defined customer profile. A true salesperson can sell anything to almost anyone, but that is often not what's best for the business. This is the *who* in W3.
- Need a defined sales process.

- Need pricing (or at least pricing parameters) to be defined. There is a known business model and pricing structure.
- Compensation is typically commission driven and title sensitive. A typical salesperson earns a base salary and the majority of their pay comes from commissions (receiving some percentage of the sale, once closed). Salespeople typically expect traditional hierarchical titles like account executive, sales manager, VP of sales, etc.
- Asks lots of questions focused on closing deals.
- Will close all business possible regardless of value fit. Going back to our BlackLocus example, our original salesperson John was closing any business he could find without regard for customer fit. He did a great job of closing *new* business, but because those customers were not right for BlackLocus, many of them churned.

Customer Development People

- Help identify and define the customer profiles.
- Help identify and define the sales process.
- Help figure out and define pricing.
- Compensation is typically base salary with an annual bonus tied to company performance.
- Rarely title sensitive.
- Ask lots of questions focused on understanding value transfer and understanding customer needs.
- Be willing to walk away from prospects when there isn't a clear value fit.

How to Find Your ICP (Ideal Customer Profile)

In Chapter 1 we discussed W3 and spent time on *who*. We developed a theory of the characteristics of our *who* and eventually put together a list of our top prospects. Now we're going to go out and see if we are right. Once we have strong conviction that our *who* is correct, we'll call that our ideal customer profile or ICP. And once we are confident in our ICP, we are one step closer to being able to scale our sales organization and revenues.

But before we get there, we need to prove, or at least get strong conviction, of our identification of our ICP. And I want to warn you that, while this work can feel a bit tedious, the risks associated with not going through this process can kill your business before you even get started.

Here is a short story from one of my portfolio companies to help illustrate the point. I invited Monica Landers to join Techstars Austin in 2016 with her company Authors.me (now called Storyfit). I knew from the moment I met Monica that she was an incredible CEO and had a great shot at building an awesome company.

A Story of Searching for Your Who

At the time, Authors.me was a marketplace for aspiring authors to post their work and for publishers to find new authors to publish. What made Authors.me special was the data science they developed so that they were able to tell an aspiring author exactly what that author needed to do, in the editing process, to develop a book that their target publisher was likely to like and publish.

Likewise, the product was able to deliver to publishers only books that fit the attributes of the books they were looking to publish, along with predictive data on how well the book would do. The real secret sauce and the actual product here was the data science. Monica and her team came out of Demand Media where they had developed similar types of technology to figure out what short form content they should publish on various websites. They knew the problem well and how to solve it and they had a strong conviction around who needed their product, writers, and publishers.

At this time they were charging both writers and publishers to be on the Authors.me platform. Writers paid a small fee to list their work and could pay an upcharge to acquire data on how they should edit their work to satisfy their target publishers. Publishers on the other hand were charged access to the marketplace. This all seemed logical, since Authors.me was solving a problem for both sides of this market, but there were some issues. Setting aside the challenge of finding aspiring writers, the authors who were approached often didn't have a lot of extra money for a listing on Authors.me, much less to pay for additional data. And since Authors.me didn't have a brand name yet or a track record of breaking new writers, it was hard to get writers to shell out money and take the leap of faith. On the other side, most publishers didn't believe technology could predict something better than an editor or were worried that the service could put editors out of work. And while many publishers would say they'd try Authors.me, very few actually were becoming customers.

Still, Monica knew the market well and knew there was a need and that there would be an eventual shift to more data-driven decision processes. At this point, Monica and I were working together at Techstars and started to question the initial theory of *who* she thought her customers would be. She felt that she was getting enough interest from publishers about Authors.me's ability to predict outcomes, and she started testing the idea that a marketplace wasn't the product, but instead a data platform for publishers was the product.

She started having some very promising conversations with all the top publishers and for a couple of months it looked as though they were moving in the right direction. Publishers seemed to be interested in a platform that would help them better predict what books should be published and how those books should be edited to better suit the target audience. But closed deals weren't moving as fast as Monica hoped. To accelerate sales into the publishing market, Monica closed a major partnership with a leading book printing company who from then on would be the primary sales channel for the company, albeit at a slow pace, given that they are still selling to publishers.

However, at this point, Monica paused and decided to see if she could disprove her current theory that publishers were her target customer. Rather than look at all the reasons why they should be, she asked herself why they might not be. She questioned whether the publishers could move fast enough in their decision making. She questioned the volume of published materials relative to the revenue they would produce, and she looked at the total universe of potential customers. And while it did look like there was a business here, her confidence in building it in a time frame that would allow her to build a profitable business looked challenging.

It was at this point that Monica questioned her *who* again and wondered who else might benefit from this product. She had thought about TV and film studios in the past, but dismissed them based on a couple of assumptions. First, she assumed they would be harder to meet than publishers. She was also concerned that the market of big studios wasn't big enough in terms of total customer potential, and, finally, she wasn't sure if finding top writers was a challenge in TV and film, as it was in the publishing world, which she knew well. She decided to test this and (by leveraging the TechStars Network) landed a few initial meetings with some studios. She very quickly learned that not only did studios have the same issue, but mistakes were much more costly, and therefore solving the problem of identifying great content by crunching data was a high priority for most studios.

Monica also learned that there were many more studios and production houses than she had originally thought. And after a few conversations she realized that not only was there a big market here, but that this segment could move faster, had more money to spend, and had a higher velocity of content that they were trying to produce. After a little more validation, Monica shifted her *who* focus, changed the company name to Storyfit (a better name for her new customer type), and directed her efforts at this segment. Fast-forward 18 months, Storyfit is working with (or soon to be working with) several of the major studios and already delivering data that is driving the content that you are likely watching on TV and in theaters.

Lessons Monica Learned from Authors.me

As you can see from this story, Monica had strong convictions about who they originally believed their ICP was; however, she and her colleagues didn't take the time to prove it. They spent months and months selling to a customer set that was never going to be able to pay enough or provide enough repeat business to build a big business. And while this customer set did have a need for the product, it wasn't strong enough for Authors.me to build a big and sustainable business with this customer set.

Fortunately Monica figured it out before the business failed and started testing new potential segments by using the customer development process to test new theories of her ICP. How did she do it?

First she took a step back and opened up her mind to being wrong about her ICP. While this may sound simple in theory, in practice it's much harder. Think about it. You've spent months or maybe longer passionately focused on building a product for a specific customer type, and in your mind, you knew exactly who that customer was. The simple act of questioning your own resolve is challenging for anyone, but especially when you've already poured months or years of work into it and likely even put yourself out there in public with this resolve. It can be a big blow to anyone's ego. But that's exactly what you have to do, you have to be open to being wrong.

Second she went back to square one and did the work to define her *who* again. In this case we were fortunate to have some data about what wasn't working, and she took the information she had about the customer she was trying to sell to into account. The three things that stood out were (1) historically, publishing was a slower moving industry; (2) data wasn't as widely used yet, compared to other industries; and (3) budgets in publishing were smaller, when existent at all, for any outside resources. Publishers didn't want to pay and most writers didn't have the money or foresight to see how this product could help them create better work, faster.

Third, she came up with a new list of potential segments and prospects within those segments to test. This included screenwriting for TV and film studios, among others.

And finally, the really tedious work began—Monica had as many conversations with potential customers as possible. Unlike the first and second time around, this time she approached each conversation to learn something rather than to sell something. She took the time to learn about internal processes, who would be the users, and who would be the decision makers (and whether it was one person with both roles). She asked about the use of technology inside the creative process, as well as budgeting for this type of technology.

And the results were great. She learned that large studios saw the emergence of Netflix as a big challenge because of their ability to, quickly, produce high-quality content for specific viewer types, while the big studios did not have the resources or DNA to build internal teams to tackle the same task. While they are great at producing great content, their model of identifying and modifying potential movies and TV shows is based more on gut instincts than on data. She also learned that there was budget set aside in the development process for research and that the Storyfit product could fall into that line item. That not only meant that there was money for the Storyfit product, but that there was money each time a new project was being considered.

She discovered several wins in these conversations. Not only would StoryFit have a head start on the technology, thanks to their work in publishing, but the book knowledge brought with it a level of trust and respect in Hollywood. Some of the most important movie franchises come from books. This deep understanding of stories across multiple media gave StoryFit a strong differentiator from other analytics companies. (And that's when the technology found its new name, from Authors.me to StoryFit.)

And with that, Storyfit had identified their *who* and was one step closer to identifying product market fit (we discuss this further on in the "Product–Market Direction and the Quest for Product–Market Fit" section).

The Methodology for Finding Your ICP

So what's the work you have to do to identify your ICP? Well, as discussed in Chapter 1, it starts with doing the *who* work. Once you have your *who* theory articulated, you are ready to start having conversations around trying to prove it right or wrong. As you recall, you've taken the time to describe *who* you think your customer will be, and you've taken the time to write down who you believe your top prospective customers will be. This is where you take that work and test it. Leverage your network and find out how you can get warm introductions to people who work with your target customers and start collecting data.

I have a very specific style and methodology here that I will describe, with the caveat that you will need to figure out what works bests for you and the industry you are focused on. There is much that you can pull from my methods; however, you will ultimately need to make the process your own.

Step 1

I use LinkedIn and the Techstars network to see where I can get warm introductions to either (a) the target job title at the company I'm trying to talk to or (b) someone senior (ideally C-level) who can point me in the right direction and even make a subsequent introduction.

Step 2

I ask for a 15-minute meeting. I make it clear that the purpose of this meeting is to share with them what I'm working on and to see if a longer meeting would be appropriate, where the longer meeting would be focused on digging in on the product idea in order to lean on their expertise in designing our product.

- Note here that while I'm using the product concept as the entry point for the conversation, inherently I'm testing the customer appetite for the concept. If they are not open to the conversation, I very politely ask, why under the pretense that it will help me figure out if I should spend any additional time working on this problem.
- Also note that when warm introductions are made, most people will give you that 15-minute meeting as it is respectful of their time and unobtrusive.
- Final note: when you are onto something, those 15 minutes consistently extend to 30 minutes or more.

Step 3

This is the data collection meeting. Sometimes this happens in that first 15-minute meeting, sometimes it's in a follow-up meeting with that person (or the person they've directed you to), and sometimes it happens over the course of a few meetings with a few different people. There isn't a wrong answer here, as long as your goal stays the same, which is to collect as much data as possible on whether you are solving a real problem for this customer and if you have the right customer type.

Here are things you should be looking for in these meetings:

1. Are the meeting attendees engaged or does it feel like they are burdened (record your gut response)?
2. How do they rank the problem (and your solution) relative to their job and the things they are working on in the near term?
3. Ask the same question, but for the company, not just their job.
4. Can you get a sense for what you expect to charge relative to what they can afford?
5. Are they pushing for time frames and follow-up (or are they even open to being an early customer)?

And here are some things to look out for in these meetings:

1. Happy ears—this is you wanting so badly to be correct that you think this potential customer is excited to buy from you when in actuality they may just be nice or not know how to say no.
2. A real problem may be mentioned, but given lower priority relative to other things they or their company needs to accomplish.
3. A real problem that needs to be solved may be mentioned, but small or no budget is currently being allocated to solving the problem (relative to your expected cost).
4. The right problem may be identified, but the wrong person in the company is present at the meeting. This is a really hard one to figure out without offending the person you are meeting with. My style is to simply be transparent from the beginning so it's possible to ask that question without it being awkward.

Now we have developed strong conviction around our *who*. We have a good idea of the problem we are solving and a good idea of who we are solving it for, and now it's time to use the customer development process to develop strong product–market direction on the quest for product–market fit.

Product–Market Direction and the Quest for Product–Market Fit

> *Our company, Chowbotics, had developed a product that could work for offices, hospitals, and restaurants as well as grocery stores. We were getting inbound interest from major brands in all these markets. Amos and Techstars advised us to identify just one beachhead market, focus on it, develop marketing and successful case studies for that beachhead market, scale sales there and later target other markets.*
>
> *Our sales team initially got excited seeing all the inbound interest from several markets and didn't follow the "focus on one beachhead market" approach. After a few months of getting overwhelmed, and taking baby steps in multiple markets instead of getting solid traction in one market, we pivoted to the "beachhead market" approach and quickly saw results. We now have hundreds of deployments in offices across the United States and Europe.*
>
> —Deepak Sekar, founder and CEO of Chowbotics

At this point you are feeling pretty good about your *who*, which means that you also feel good that the problem you thought you were solving is actually a problem worth solving. This is a great step in the right direction but just because you know your *who* and have validated the problem doesn't mean you have product–market fit, it just means that you have a reasonably strong idea that a group of people have a problem worth solving.

Understanding Product–Market Fit

Chances are that if you've read any startup literature, pitched your business to investors, or even just talked to other startup people about your company that you are familiar with the concept of product–market fit. In the case that you are not, this is a really important concept to understand and internalize. Wikipedia's definition of product–market fit is the degree to which a product satisfies a strong market demand. To simplify it, I tell my portfolio companies that you know you have achieved product–market fit when some group of people can't (or don't want to) live without your product. Important to note here is that just because you have product–market fit doesn't mean you have the right product to build a big company. If that group of people is very small or not willing to pay what you need to charge, then your company can still fail; however, without product–market fit you will have zero chance of building a big company because it essentially means that no one needs your product (or at least for any sustained period of time).

It can take months or even years to fully achieve product–market fit. Once you've achieved it, it's likely that you've built or at least are on the way to building a really big business. Some great examples of companies who have achieved incredible product–market fit are Salesforce.com, Apple Computer Company, and Google. These companies all have customers who either need their products, or prefer their products compared to their competitor's products because it satisfies their unique needs. And while some of that can be attributed to brand loyalty now, that brand promise was built on the back of achieving product–market fit for their target customer set.

Knowing Your Product–Market Direction

Long before you achieve product–market fit, however, you need to get product–market direction. I've talked about this concept for several years. Upon the writing of this book, I did a lot of research to figure out where I originally heard the concept but couldn't locate anything. I don't believe I'm the first person to use this concept and for the sake of this book, if I'm not giving someone the proper attribution, please accept my apologies and thanks for the great concept.

Product–market direction is exactly that. It means you've identified *who* you are targeting for the problem you are attempting to solve and that you have directional indicators that the product you are building is heading in the right direction.

There is a very important attribute that we need to tease out here and a key differentiator between a salesperson and the person in your organization doing customer development. If you go back to the "Sales versus Customer Development" section, you'll recall that a salesperson needs a reasonably well-defined product to sell. And you'll also recall that until you have that well-defined product, you are in customer development mode. There is an aspect of this role that is a hybrid of a product person and a salesperson. It's the role of the person doing customer development to keep searching for those directional points, and it's a hard and important balance to strike.

Think of it like this, the person doing customer development needs to have enough of a product mindset to ask questions, listen really well, and direct both customers and your company's team to build the right product while also being able to identify when a product threshold has been met. That customer development person can actually turn an exploratory conversation into a sale and revenue for your company.

This rarely happens as one step and almost never happens with the first iteration of a product. Much more frequently, it is series of product iterations (sometimes dozens or more) over a longer period of time (months and years). Sometimes people refer to these iterations as pivots, which isn't necessarily wrong but the concept of pivot has adopted a pretty specific definition and negative connotation to "whatever you were doing was wrong, so you are going to do something completely different."

I think about it more like sailing. When you sail, you know your starting point and you know your ending point. What the sailor doesn't always know is which way the wind is blowing and how it will shift while trying to get from point A to point B. Sometimes the wind is at your back, sometimes it's on one of your sides, and sometimes you are sailing straight into the wind. If you are out for a long enough trip it's likely the wind will change several times, meaning you'll need to change the direction and type of sail you will need. Your sailboat almost never goes directly straight and instead, in order to go from point A to point B, you and your crew will need to tack. This means the front of your boat is going left and right and left and right in order to "head straight" to your destination. Sometimes those tacks are very small and sometimes they are very large.

You can think about achieving product–market fit as a destination. And along the way you are tacking your business by looking for the product–market direction.

Every great company out there has gone through several iterations taking them from directional point to directional point. Yelp started as a social network asking friends for recommendations, Groupon was originally a platform for charitable causes, YouTube was originally a video dating service, and Slack was a feature of the video game Glitch (see https://www.entrepreneur.com/article/308975). In all four cases the CEOs of these companies recognized a couple of things. First was that their *who* was a group worth addressing, next that there was a problem that needed to be solved, and also that the product they originally brought to market had attractive attributes but was not exactly the right product to build a big company.

How Slack Tacked Its Way to Success

Let's talk about Slack because not only do I love this example but it is a great example of a company that continues to tack in order to *maintain* product–market fit (because, yes, it's something you can lose, too, if you don't continue to innovate). Originally, Slack was nothing more than a feature inside the video game Glitch. While the game was reasonably successful, the founders noticed something interesting, which was the way that their players socialized with one another in the game, which was to say, a lot and in depth.

The founders had the foresight to pull the feature out of the game and create Slack. That in and of itself is a big pivot, but that isn't what we are going to focus on here. What happened next is what I find truly remarkable and a great example of looking for product–market directional points as a way to continue to grow.

Today a large number of businesses use Slack as a communication tool within the company, in teams within the company, with their customers, and in many other ways. But in order to get there Slack had to listen to what their users were telling them (directly and indirectly) and continually evolve the product. They needed to add ways to keep communication separate and secure: they needed to have desktop and mobile experiences as well as experience options for non-Slack users so that their customers could leverage the Slack platform. And now, after dozens and dozens of product iterations, Slack is one of the most widely used business communications platforms around.

* * *

Identifying product–market direction is difficult and sometimes feels like one of the most tedious parts of building a company. You have a strong conviction of *who* your customer is and you know deep in your bones the problem you are solving. And on your quest to find product–market fit it's likely you will have many iterations of your product. Some will be awesome and others you will simply throw away. And while those times often feel like wasted time and work they are actually crucial for you to get from point A to point B and ultimately achieve product–market fit.

Now It's Your Turn to Start the Customer Development Process

We will break the customer development process into five steps:

1. Create a list of initial targets—this should be a combination of warm introductions and people you do not know.
2. Create a list of questions you need answered and data you need to collect to support your W3 theory.
3. Schedule interview/meetings.
4. Collect and analyze the data.
   - Ask questions.
   - Close beta customers.
   - Ask more questions.
5. Refine/repeat.

Chapter 3

Your Sales Process—The Road to Repeatability

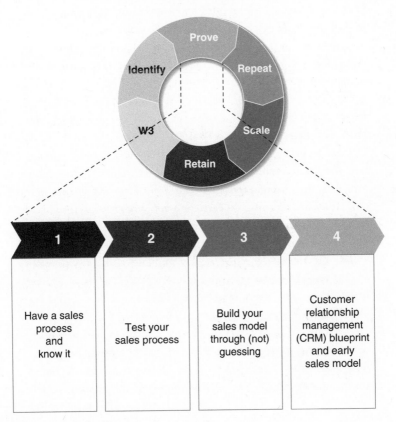

Figure 3.1 Your Sales Process

Process is something that people associate with structure and bureaucracy—but I see it as a liberator and creativity enabler. Why is there such a difference in thought? One of the things that is interesting about process is that, in my opinion, it's meant to create the flywheel for repeatability so that you are free to work on important, high priority, and nonrepeatable "things."

My third and fourth jobs were as a network administrator. I fell in love with UNIX and the concept of making a world of processes that just worked so that I could focus on the real problems that need a solution. My first business, Net Daemons Associates, was named in support of process. A daemon is a program (kind of) that runs in UNIX whose only purpose is to keep things working. My business partner lived by the philosophy that if you were going to do something more than once, you should write a program for it so that you could just push the button the next time.

Sales is an art and much of it is a formula. There is a beginning a middle and an end to every sale. If you are doing sales correctly, you are using strong brand and messaging which needs to be repeated and amplified so that every person that is being sold is getting the same message. The art is making sure that there is a strong core of process—how do you pitch, what tools do you use, what stories do you tell, what is your pricing, how do you negotiate—with a personal and emotional wrapper that humanizes and engages. If you don't have the process, you will spend less time on that bespoke, emotional element, and, as a result, sell less.

I think one of the most important parts of business is listening. With sales, you need to listen to what your customer is in pain over so that you can propose the right solution for them. You have time to be focused on listening when you have the ordinary and the day-to-day delivered by the engine of process.

Process is a liberator. It lets you put definition and reliability, accountability and efficiency around things that should happen in a repeatable and accountable way and then lets you use the rest of your time to be creative, innovative and work on big picture issues.

—Jenny Lawton, COO Techstars

Why Having and Knowing Your Sales Process Is Important

It took me a little while to get started on writing this chapter. There are a number of reasons for this; first of all, writing (or reading) about process isn't typically very exciting for many founders and sales leaders, who prefer to be in the real world, creating and doing more faster. Process can sometimes feel very boring and tedious (or what big companies do, not startups). I'm personally not one to create process simply for the sake of having a process, however, my experience (and the experience of almost any sales leader in a well-run sales organization) is that one of the keys to selling more faster is a well-defined sales process (Figure 3.1).

The other reason that this chapter took me a little while to get started is because there are so many resources out there already that discuss "the sales process." If you Google "sales process" there are 2.4 billion results. If you Google "books on sales process," it narrows your search to 393 million search results.

I don't want to waste your time providing the same information you can get in literally millions of other places; however, I do recognize how crucial *your* sales process will be to *your* ability to scale *your* sales organization and *your* company. Instead, what we will do in this chapter is to use the work we've done up until this point and start to tease out the first iteration of *your* sales process.

I also want to stress "first iteration." Creating your sales process is a lot like being at the beach and digging a hole near the water. Once you hit water in your hole it's nearly impossible to make much progress because the hole keeps filling up with water, caving in the sides, and you don't make nearly as much progress as you think you should. Getting to the point (at some time in the future) where you have a truly repeatable sales process will feel a lot like digging that hole. You'll have many iterations of your process as you learn more about the sale and what is important to your customer relative to your company. You'll have iterations as your product matures and starts to fill in gaps where you previously needed process. And you'll also have iterations as you hire more salespeople and learn how different people and selling styles inform the process. Finally, you'll have sales process iterations as you define (and change) what is important to the company in terms of selling and reporting. This chapter deals only with your first sales process iteration, but without this first iteration you'll have nothing to iterate on (and no path to your repeatable sales process).

Now I realize there are people out there who love and thrive on creating process. If you are one of those people, then this chapter should be a quick read and affirmation to your thinking.

If you aren't a process lover, however, I want you to rest assured that I've done my best to keep this chapter interesting while also giving you very tangible steps to teasing your (first crack at a) sales process out of the work you've done from the book up to this point.

I also want to reiterate that this is not a chapter about "what a sales process is." While I'll provide you with a simple definition shortly, this chapter is about taking the work from the first few chapters of this book and using it to begin building your sales organization on the road to finding YOUR repeatable sales process. The reason this is important is because without a repeatable sales process, you don't have a repeatable sales process. Yes, you read that correctly, that's not a typo. Stop and think about that for just five seconds.

It is impossible to build a scalable sales organization without a repeatable sales process because there isn't any sale to (knowingly) repeat, which means you don't have a product that can scale to many organizations. You won't be able to hire and retain salespeople because they won't know what it is that they are selling, how to sell it, or to whom. Additionally, having a repeatable sales process gives you the ability to model out sales growth so you know how your hiring will affect revenue and cash burn. And finally, without a repeatable sales process, which enables all of the above, it'll be much harder to win the confidence of your investors (or future investors).

More specifically in this chapter we will discuss two basic methods. First, we will learn how to tease out your (first iteration of your) sales process from the work we did with W3 and through the customer development process. Within that, we'll talk about the importance of a customer relationship management (CRM) system, which I strongly encourage, to make your job easier. Next, we will talk about and start to do some work around sales modeling so that you can begin to put all of this work together and start growing your business. In the final part of this chapter

I've included two exercises so that you can build out your sales process and build an early sales model.

Defining the Sales Process

So what is a sales process? A sales process is a repeatable set of steps your sales team takes with a prospect to move them from early stage to a closed customer. A good sales process helps your reps consistently close deals by giving them a framework to follow. Figure 3.2 is a visual representation of a sales process:

In Figure 3.2 I've intentionally used the visual of a funnel. The list of "steps" is what's crucial here, but I'm killing two birds with one stone. You see that aside from understanding the steps of your sales process, your sales process will also inform your sales funnel, which are the steps your prospects move from lead to closed customer. In each step some prospects will fall out and others will move on (hence the narrowing funnel). Understanding both why prospects fall out as well as move on is critical to growing your business, coaching your salespeople, and understanding what is working and what is not on your path to building a repeatable sales process.

Figure 3.2 Sales Funnel
Source: Courtesy of Austin Dressen.

Seeing the Benefits of a Repeatable Process

I'm on the board of a company called ScaleFactor. ScaleFactor provides automated accounting and bookkeeping services to small and medium businesses. I first invested in ScaleFactor in 2017 when they joined Techstars Austin. At that time, the business looked more like a services business than a software business. They were doing about $1.5 million in revenue and had a loose idea of who they thought their customer was. They had only one salesperson in addition to the CEO. One of ScaleFactor's main goals coming into Techstars Austin was to become a scaleable software company. While in the three-month program, we worked on identifying our W3 and proving it through the customer development process.

Shortly after Techstars, we hired David Loia as our chief revenue officer. He took that initial work and has since developed a highly repeatable sales process, which has resulted in exponential revenue growth. The work we did in Techstars was foundational to attracting David to ScaleFactor because it gave him a decent understanding of what we did, for who and why, which gave him the confidence and understanding to accept the job and start building out the sales organization. I've been extremely impressed with the work David has done at ScaleFactor specially around putting a repeatable sales process in place.

Here is an excerpt from David on what he did and why it proved to be critical to growing ScaleFactors revenue exponentially over the following 18+ months, which has resulted in incredible sales growth as well as raising over $40 million from both Canaan and Bessemer.

> It is imperative to reinvigorate the sales process much more frequently than a founder team might realize, and target revenue tipping points roughly on Fibonacci's sequence, that is, $1 million, $2 million, $3 million, $5 million, $8 million, $13 million, and so on.
>
> Nothing that is working well at each revenue tipping point will be sufficient to get you to the next one.

Massive change is a constant necessity, all the time, especially at high-growth, since you will be blowing through tipping points every few quarters. The second something starts working, pour gas on it, because you are sure to be changing it for something better.

At pre–$1 million in revenue, founders are immersed in the daily struggle of testing markets and ICPs, honing messaging, building MVP, and generally also doing the prospecting and selling themselves by necessity. When the smolder shows some small flames, the founders proceed to hire some dedicated salespeople to fan the fragile flame. But then, they find that what they learned to get the first $1 million of revenue doesn't work well to get to $3 million, and none of it works at the $5 million tipping point.

—**David Loia, chief revenue officer at ScaleFactor**

Teasing Out *Your* First Sales Process

In chapter 1 we talked about developing a strategy so that you can start the customer development process. Then in Chapter 2 we took that work and applied it to the customer development process with the goal of being able to move from customer development to sales by firmly identifying our ICP. The other byproduct of the customer development process we haven't discussed yet is the sales process.

My experience has been that, although there are many similarities between sales processes, no two are really alike *and* it takes a solid customer development process and a clear understanding of your ICP before you can define the process that optimizes for your business.

In this section, we will talk about how to tease out your sale process, through understanding your sales funnel. In that process we will also touch on some basic tools to build and manage your team. Then in the "Building Your Sales Model through (Not)

Guessing" section, we will take that information and build an early sales model.

> What I avoid as a pro CRO, and you should, too, if you want to scale fast: The "strategy of convenience." Meaning doing something because it's obvious and easy. It's a method of decision making that is a necessity in the under $1 million tipping point and therefore a darling of many founders.
>
> At later tipping points, however, and especially post A, if the path you're on happens to be the easiest one to execute in the moment (a.k.a. the strategy of convenience), it's probably wrong for high growth. Growth is always hard and high growth takes a lot of hard work plus flawless execution. That's not easy, so the strategy of convenience is likely going to lead you away from high growth, not toward it.
>
> Likewise, how things were at previous tipping points, however nostalgic they might be for the founders, mean little for the new players, whose incremental ideas and efforts are levered exponentially to scale up to future tipping points. Looking backwards distracts from cementing the vision of where the company is going, and the changes that need to be made to get there. Historians inadvertently rally the more tenured teammates against the massive and frequent change that scaling up requires, usually with phraseology like "This is how we did it when we started the company." Scaling up is about making the new people succeed quickly, never perpetuating the status quo.
>
> ——**David Loia, chief revenue officer at ScaleFactor**

Focusing on Your Sales Funnel

Let's start with your sales funnel. If you ask most businesspeople, they will tell you that the sales funnel is simply a list of companies you think will become customers and where they are in the process. This simply is not true; the real answer is much deeper than that.

I think about the sales funnel as a visual representation of your sales process that tells you what work you need to do in order to drive revenue, as well as the priority and importance of that work.

A great funnel tells you not only the stage a given prospect is in your process but also who you need to be talking to (inside and outside the company), the materials you need to be preparing, the questions you need to be asking, what you need to do to close the deal and the things you need to know to keep your customer satisfied and delighted after the sale is closed.

When you first kick off your customer development process it's pretty hard to have any idea of your sales process or what your funnel will look like. What I usually tell people is to pick four to six stages that feel right and just start tracking and recording data. Some common first-pass stages are:

Lead > First Contact > Demo > Proposal > Negotiation > Close

From a nomenclature perspective, something like that might always be your stage names but what changes is what you learn and know about each stage. It's also common to add/change/delete some of this as you learn more about your actual process.

For example, let's use the negotiation stage. For a simple sale (or B2C sale), negotiation may not be a stage because there is nothing to negotiate. For a slightly more complex product or selling to a midmarket customer, you may need some simple negotiating with your business buyer and you may need to build tools and rules for your salespeople to follow so they are empowered to close business or you may decide that you always bring in a manager for negotiating. Then on a more complex sale, and especially if selling to an enterprise, there is also a procurement process that often restarts some (or all) of the negotiation and may bring up new points, which may change who on your team works with each person at your prospects company (including bringing lawyers in). Depending on how you define your stages, this may be part of the negotiation stage or a stage all by itself. As you can see, with this one stage, *negotiation*, we've defined several different ways to think about it that will dictate the process you build out.

Each one of these stages is not just a simple word, but think about each as a more complex concept of where your prospect is in your funnel, For example, let's look at another company in my portfolio, Allstacks.

Allstacks: Finding the Right Sales Process

Allstacks is a data and analytics platform for developers (and their managers) to understand the data and metrics behind their development process. In other words, similar to Sales or Marketing, Allstacks gives companies insight into how their development projects are moving through their development cycles.

When Allstacks joined Techstars Austin in January 2018, they had about a dozen (early) customers and defined their sales process as

Lead > Demo > Customer

When I look at that funnel, it tells me:

1. Identify a company as a good lead.
2. Give a demo of their product.
3. Win or lose that prospect as a customer.

What it does not tell me is:

1a. Whether there is a difference between lead types.
1b. How a prospect moves from lead to a demo.
1c. Anything about lead types.

It also doesn't tell me:

2a. What happens after a demo to move a prospect along.
2b. What happens if the prospect says no during the demo.

And while there might be something nice about such a simple funnel it doesn't answer any of the questions along the way as to why your prospect is or isn't progressing through your funnel.

Here Hersh, CEO of Allstacks, is telling you firsthand about his experience figuring out their funnel:

> When we first started Allstacks we agonized over forming the sales funnel. What stages should we have? How should they be defined? Why do they matter? We had a ton of questions and were struggling to find answers. Being engineers,

we had a certain disconnect with the sales process. The big learning was when we realized the sales process was more about throughput than any particular deal. It was tough to reconcile against software development because you can't just say as long as 15% of the features we define at the top of the funnel ("prospects") get completed and delivered ("closed won") the software will work. The particular features matter a lot.

With sales, we realized the buyers within our target persona were substantially equivalent so we needed to optimize our conversion through the sales funnel.

Still armed with a litany of questions in hand, we decided the best thing to do was simply embrace the questions and define our sales funnel stages as a series of questions. What do we need to ask to determine why a buyer makes it to the next phase? As we answered each successive question it revealed the next set of questions we needed to answer to build our sales funnel. Eventually, all of the questions had been answered and we knew where to focus. At a high level the questions started out quite simply:

1. Will anyone respond to us?

   We had acquired a list of leads so we segmented the list, and tried different value propositions against them. Eventually, we found one that worked for us and we started to engage our prospects. Interestingly enough, it had little to do pushing a value proposition and everything to do with engaging a human. We asked, "What is a metric that you care about measuring for your software team?" This led to a massive increase in conversion to the next question:

2. Will anyone take a demo?

   This question was fairly easily to validate. Once we were successfully able to engage our customers as a result of answering question 1, the demo came fairly quickly, our buyer persona was curious and always wanted to see the product. However, once in a demo, where to go from there? This led to our first diverging path. A lot of the buyers asked for access to a demo account or a free trial. What we found, consistently, is that the demo account fell flat and killed enthusiasm. The learning was that buyers had to see their own data in Allstacks, not dummy data. So we went onwards.

3. Will they sign up for a trial?

Luckily, in the mid-market buyer development and analytics tool space, this was pretty table stakes. Everyone expected a trial, however—

4. Will they convert to paid?

This was the tricky part. Wherever you can, the recommendation is always, don't give out free trials. This becomes challenging when buyers have been trained by the market to purchase in a certain way, as we experienced. So we had to search for the magic moment when a series of actions taken within Allstacks led to teams using the product consistently, and Allstacks became sticky. For us, when teams use Allstacks to drive their daily standups and run their retrospectives we achieve that magic moment. Guiding our buyers through that process helps drive our conversion.

By defining our sales funnel as a series of questions we were able to understand where we had uncertainty. Anytime we couldn't answer a question we knew we were lacking data and needed to become more granular on the questions we were asking. This helped us tailor a sales funnel tightly to a critical path we knew worked for us without trying to arbitrarily match a generic funnel to our sales motion.

—Hersh Tapadia, CEO of Allstacks

Working with Hersh was a great example of figuring out and understanding the sales process. First of all, Hersh was a developer at heart so he openly welcomed the concept of a process. Not to mention there is a direct correlation between the sales process (and need for it) with Allstacks and what he was building for developers. Figuring out and focusing on what the Allstacks process should be helped him think about how to develop the Allstacks product as well. Now, almost a year later and with a more mature process, their sales numbers are several orders of magnitude greater, they have better insight into who is a real prospect in their funnel, how long that sale will take to close, and how much they can expect from each sale. Not only does this give Hersh and the team confidence about growing the business (and future hiring), it gave potential investors the confidence in Hersh, the team, and the process to invest into a very healthy seed round (giving Hersh and team more financial ability to execute and sell more faster).

Using a CRM to Track Customers and Data

Okay, so let's go back to the beginning—what are the steps you think you'll need to go through to close a sale, then start tracking and recording data? What I mean by this is that you'll want to start tracking, at minimum,

1. The number of prospects in any given stage.
2. The time a prospect sits in any given stage/how long it takes to move from stage to stage.
3. What needs to happen in any stage for that prospect to move to the next stage?
4. Why prospects move (or don't move) from stage to stage.
5. Proposed revenue before a prospect becomes a customer versus revenue once that prospect becomes a customer.
6. The win/lose rate at each stage.

In order to do this well, most people (and I) highly recommend a customer relationship management (CRM) system. If you aren't already familiar, a CRM is a software tool used by most companies to track the entire lifespan of their customers (from prospect through the day when they no longer want to be a customer and become a prospect again). While using a spreadsheet can work in the earliest days, it very quickly ages, doesn't provide a good ability to track data or build reports and it doesn't scale as you add people.

At a minimum I'd start with something like Streak or Freecrm .com. There are tons and tons of CRMs out there. The most common is Salesforce.com, which is a very powerful CRM but can also work well for early stage companies. The two challenges I have with Salesforce are cost and complexity. It's a lot of work for an early stage company just trying to figure out who they are.

At Techstars Austin, we currently use Airtable. Upon writing this chapter, we've only used it for about a year but I love it because it's easy to customize, very flexible and easily allows for both multiple customer types (great when you are learning or more mature) and making changes to process and flow on the fly. If you do not already have a CRM you like, I would recommend trying Airtable. If there is already a CRM you've used in the past and like, just use that one. There isn't really a wrong answer here, other than to not use one at all.

Once you pick a CRM, set aside half a day or so and set up the first iteration of what you think your process will be—think of this as your V1, just like in the software development process. Take the time to think through *how* you will be using it. Here is a quick step by step to get you started. Keep in mind both that this process *will* evolve over time and that the process for your company will be different than most other businesses out there.

Step 1: Prospect Types

If you think you might have different prospect or customer types, then try to take this into account from the beginning. Different types could be enterprise customers, medium-sized businesses, or resellers. It could also be industry specific.

Step 2: Steps

Add in all the steps you believe you need to track, based on what you currently know about your sales process. If you aren't sure where to start, then you can use my example (*Lead > First Contact > Demo > Proposal > Negotiation > Close*). Make sure you have a definition (ideally in your CRM, for all to see) of what each step means to your company.

Step 3: Reporting

Set up some basic reporting on what you currently think you need to be tracking. Some common items are: projected sales revenue by month and quarter and weighted based on stage, time for prospects to move from stage to stage, stalled prospects, closed win/lose report. Note: This is one step you can punt on for a few weeks if this is out of your comfort zone. I'll cover this in "Evaluating Progress" section.

Step 4: Use It

This is the most important step—*use it*! Set an example for the entire company. The earlier and more accurately you have this information, the better positioned you are to sell more faster and communicate with your company, customers, and investors.

* * *

One important note to keep in mind for setting up your CRM: when you set up fields for collecting data, think about what needs to be free form versus what data needs to be cleaner data (i.e. choices) when you collect it. The more you can have defined fields, the easier it will be for you to understand the data and make projections; however, sometimes you need some free-form fields to record, for example, *why* someone has decided to buy or not to buy your product. You don't likely have enough information yet to formalize the "why," so collect it free form and then in time change it to an option field once you have enough data to understand why.

Once you do this, you probably don't need to check in on your process more often than quarterly or whenever you learn something substantially new and obvious that needs to be added. Finally the most important thing, which I will say again: *use it*! Be diligent about taking notes and updating statuses. It takes a little work to build this muscle, but it will pay off in dividends because, aside from the great data you will have, it builds it into your culture from day one.

Evaluating Progress

Okay, so you've set up your CRM and started inputting data. Maybe you even have a couple of other people calling customers.

After about three to six weeks, set aside half a day to think about and build out your first set of reports. Think about what you've personally learned about the prospects you've been calling, how they are moving through the funnel, and take your first stab at the data that you believe are the biggest indicators of learning how to close business. Then pick three to five metrics at maximum. These will be your first set of sales key performance indicators (KPIs). (Note: Keep in mind that this is different than your business KPIs; only one or two of these will likely be part of those KPIs).

Once you have your sales KPIs, it's time to create a weekly meeting with the key internal folks. At a later stage company, this is likely a manager and teams, separate managers and directors and VPs and up to CEO. At an early stage company, the CEO is likely one of the people (or the only person) doing customer development. It's still crucial to meet with key stakeholders, both to share learning and also to assign accountability. If you are super early and there are only a few people in your company, then invite everyone, including your developers, so they have visibility into what you are doing and how your mutual work impacts each other's ability to be more successful. There isn't really a wrong group of people here to be included, with the caveat that each person should understand how their work mutually impacts the other's. Groups can get too big, so as your company grows, try to limit the meeting only to key stakeholders as time goes on though I encourage you to share pipelines openly so anyone in the company can see progress.

Building Your Sales Model through (Not) Guessing

As an entrepreneur I was always comfortable with uncertainty and always felt that it was a necessary trait of a successful founder. But I now realize that while it is impossible to plan the trajectory of an early stage company, that you can remove a lot of uncertainty with a great financial model.

Let me be specific. I am not talking about "projections": the only thing we know for sure about projections is that they are wrong. I am talking about a bottoms-up financial model that has assumptions as inputs and attempts to create a mathematical representation of how your business works. If each sales rep can make X calls and close Y percent of them, then if you know the number of reps you have each month and the size of the average sale, you can calculate the sales, salaries, and commissions fairly accurately.

If you want more sales, then you need more reps. In this model will come more expenses and more revenue—it represents what actually will happen. Contrast that with a "model" that just shows a consistent rate of growth (10 percent month over month, for example), but does not account for any of the expenses or work that it takes to get that growth.

Once you have a model, you should update it each month, updating your assumptions first to reflect reality more closely and then tweak the formulas if you need to make it even more accurate going forward. If you do this consistently it is almost like having a crystal ball into your business's future.

——Troy Henikoff, managing director, MATH
Venture Partners

The final part of this chapter is building an early sales model. A sales model is a general framework that defines an organization's high-level approach to selling and is a mathematical representation of what you project your sales to be using historical data layered with future/new expectations (ideally also based on data).

You likely don't have nearly enough data to fully understand the sales process and typical sales cycle, much less to create meaningful long-term revenue projections. That being said, *now* is the time to build discipline around being a metrics-driven sales organization. This is important for several reasons, for one creating that culture early on helps with hiring, training, and growing your sales organization. Another reason is that as you grow, your current and future investors and advisors will need this information to understand how they can be helpful and when to invest (more) money. The more you understand your process and can talk to your sales funnel that is backed up with data, the more confidence you build with them for future support. Finally and most important, it's the blueprint for how you will run your business so that you have a deep understanding of how to grow and make money.

In the previous section we mention that many startup people don't love process; likewise, most startup founders or sales leaders would like to avoid building sales models. That said, at the end of the day every business is a math equation and the best founders and sales leaders I know have all developed (if they didn't already have it) a love/hate relationship with digging in and building their own models. Over time as your company grows, you'll likely have staff to help with this task, but early on I believe it is critical for each department head to build their own models because it both forces and demonstrates a deep understanding of what is happening in your department and helps instruct the rest of the company on how to work together to grow.

Early modeling shouldn't be hard, especially if you've done the work to create a meaningful sales funnel that you follow in your CRM. Everything around modeling in this part going forward assumes you've done that work.

So let's get to it. Your company's size and how many customers you currently have will largely dictate the complexity and accuracy of your model. While you do want to be as complete and accurate as possible, it's more important to distinguish between what you know as *fact* (using data) and what you *believe* to be true (labeled as assumptions).

Let's step back and look at everything we've discussed so far. This is all the information you have, so far, that will help you develop your sales model.

First let's start with W3 and the customer development process. By now you should have a directional idea of who your customers will be and a very early idea of your sales process. Also, it should be pretty easy to identify all your expenses associated directly with sales. This includes ongoing costs like salary commission, materials, and potential travel and one-time costs like a computer. That is all the information you need to build the first pass on your first sales model.

For those of you who have never built a model before, here are some tips:

1. Even if you are not familiar with using formulas, the ones you'll need for this first model will be pretty simple. Wherever you are doing any math (within or between cells), take

the time to learn how to use formulas. We won't go into this here, but between tutorials in any spreadsheet and Google, it should be pretty easy to figure out.

2. Next, build out models by month. Your columns will be months while your revenue and expense drivers will be in rows. Start by building out two years, but also know that each month further out will be less and less accurate, because we simply don't have enough information yet. The purpose here is not for accurate projections, but to build a model we can start tracking against to help us learn how to more accurately project in the future. The reason I say two years (versus one or three or more) at this early stage is simply because of the discipline in thinking into the future. Anything beyond two years (and really even just one year) is just a guess, but the mental exercise of starting to think about the future is what we're looking for here.

3. Then, lay out your framework on a spreadsheet. Label the months (starting at column B or C) at the top, then down column A put in what your revenue drivers are, followed by a line break and then your expense drivers. These are just the labels, the data will go in the cells by month.

4. Finally, make a pot of coffee, carve out four hours where you won't be interrupted, and get to work. Expect that you may have a couple of false starts (especially if you don't build models all the time). Don't let those frustrate you, they are a crucial part of the process in learning and figuring out how to actually manage your business.

At SurePayroll we had originally used benchmarks from Paychex, a public company that was also targeting small businesses, to drive many of our assumptions. One of the key assumptions is the number of employees per client company. You charge on a per employee basis, and so larger companies meant more revenue. We looked at the data from Paychex and assumed our average client would have 14 employees. It seemed appropriate.

As we started operating and building out client base, it quickly became apparent that our clients were skewing smaller, averaging just over six employees each.

When we first realized this, we thought we were done. Revenue would be a fraction of what we had predicted and we would have trouble making ends meet. But, since we had a detailed, bottoms-up financial model, we were able to update the assumption for the average number of employees per client to 6.5 and immediately see exactly how revenue and expenses were impacted.

Sure, we had less revenue, but we also had lower expenses—fewer ACH fees, less customer support, and so on. In the end, the financial model gave us the confidence that in spite of the fact that reality was less than half of what we had initially predicted, that we still had a viable business, and we pushed forward. Ironically, 10 years later Paychex acquired SurePayroll for well over $100 million, and it became their solution of choice for the small end of the SMB market.

—**Troy Henikoff, managing director,**
MATH Venture Partners

Your CRM Blueprint and Early Sales Model

There are two exercises for this section. The first is quick and is around building your first sales funnel and the first stab at your sales process. The second is building your first model. You won't be able to do this until you've completed the first exercise (and likely for a few weeks after).

Exercise 1: Defining your Sales Funnel

Step 1: Pick Your CRM

If you've worked with CRMs before and you already have a comfort level with one, go with that. If you've never worked with a CRM before and/or are looking for something very easy and cheap (or free) the two I recommend are either Streak or Freecrm.com. Streak is by far the easiest CRM I've used in terms of set-up, plus it plugs right into Gmail. Gmail integration has benefits in terms of pulling contacts out of your emails.

The downside to Streak is it's not great for reporting or time-stamped note taking. Streak can be a good place to start if it's just you or a couple of people at most. Once you have more than three to four sellers you'll want to graduate to something more robust. Freecrm.com is another good one and it's free for the first couple of users. It's a little more complex to set up (more like setting up Salesforce) but you'd be able to use it for a bit longer. My team recently started using Airtable and really love it. It's a bit more on the complex side and isn't free but so far we are very happy with the capabilities.

Step 2: Sales Stages

Write down four to eight stages you believe will be part of the sales process. Some examples are: *Lead > FirstContact > Demo > Proposal > Negotiation > Close*. If you need a refresher, you can reference the "Teasing Out *Your* First Sales Process" section.

1. Next to each, describe *why* this should be a stage.
2. Next write down three to five pieces of information you need to confidently move that prospect to the next phase and the questions you'll need to ask to gain that information, for example:
   1. Who are you talking to (title and responsibility)?
   2. Do they have buying or influencing power? Note: If the answer to this is "no," it's important to identify who does. You will not be able to ultimately make a sale without getting that person's buy-in.
   3. Is there a known pain?
   4. How are they currently solving the pain?
   5. How does your solution rank in their normal workday prioritization?
   6. Is there a budget, even if it's already being spent?
3. Then write down how long you believe a prospect will be in each stage and what you believe you need to do to move that prospect to the next stage.

It's important to take mental note as you move into this section of the exercise—the result of the answers to the following questions will give you a deep understanding of what it will take you to move a prospect from a noncustomer to a customer.

Step 3: Implementation

Finally, create that process in your CRM.

Call your first prospect and test the process/make tweaks if necessary. When you first get started, the process may feel either a little clunky or a bit sparse in terms of what you know, learn, and understand about how a sale is made. Once you have a more mature process it should feel very intuitive to anyone selling your product. By this I mean that the steps in your process or obvious points where any person selling your product is taking a natural pause before moving to the next step. An obvious example might be when you go from delivering a demo to someone asking for pricing—it's pretty clear that the prospect is moving along.

Your business will have its own natural breaking points, and as you refine your sales process, assuming you are doing the work to create a repeatable process, these breaking points will be intuitive and occur naturally. Before then, however, the best you can do is put a stake in the ground where you believe these points are, test them, and refine them as you learn more.

Exercise 2: Building Your First Sales Model (First Pass after Four to Six Weeks)

If you've been in market selling (or doing customer development), how long does it take you to close prospects from initial outreach? You can use the following questions as a guide to be more efficient. If you are not yet in the market selling, then the best you can do now is take an educated guess based on the data you do have. It's perfectly okay to be wrong; what's more important is that you have a point of view to test against. I strongly encourage you to not skip this part if you aren't in the market yet. There are many advantages to collecting this data early on, in terms of how your efforts progress as well as how you communicate to potential investors, to give them confidence in the sales process.

Step 1: How Long Will It Take to Get an Initial Contact to Take a Meeting?

This may seem obvious but there is no better way to get a meeting than from a warm introduction. But also keep in mind that warm introductions will move faster earlier on in the process. As you get into the process there should be a leveling point for all prospects. When I first started as a salesperson at HotJobs, very few people made initial contact over email and I spent most of my days on the phone. As the years have gone by, it's become pretty standard for initial introductions to happen over email. If you aren't getting a warm introduction, consider other sites; for example, I've had a lot of success using LinkedIn. Lists can work, too, but when you are in the earlier stages it's likely you don't have budget for a list (and especially when you are still proving your *who* in your W3).

Step 2: What Time Frame Are You Working through Each Stage?

How long do you spend in each stage, is it hours? Days? Weeks? Months? This can vary widely depending on the type of product you have, the type of prospect you are talking to, and the price point of your product. I've been a part of the sales of SaaS products that are sold in a single phone call and others that have 12-plus-month sales cycles. The longer the sales cycle, the more important it is to have an understanding of how long each step should take, so you can more accurately track progress of your prospects. This also helps you to know when things may be heading off track.

Step 3: Are There Certain Things That Hang You Up in a Given Stage?

You may get lots of prospects excited when giving a demo of your product, but then not hear from them again. Or you might receive lots of requests for pricing and proposals, ending up with lots of stalled prospects. There will be other examples of stalling that will be specific to your business. Pay close attention when looking for these hurdles. They are the key to understanding how to grow sales, because they unlock potential issues in your product, pricing, pitch, customer type, and so on. And while many founders (and salespeople) want to bulldoze their way through these issues, understanding what they are and how to overcome then with repeatability is crucial to *selling more faster* and building a big and long-lasting company.

Step 4: What Other People (on Your Team and Prospects Team) Need to Be Involved to Close a Sale?

Depending on the type of sales you have, you may need to bring others into the process. For example, for a simple transactional sale it may just be you; however, if the sale is more technical or if your product touches several parts of your prospect's organization, then there will be others involved. This could range from other department heads like the VP of engineering or VP of marketing or even someone from the C-suite.

Step 5: Can You Determine the Cost of a Sale?

What are the tools and unique items that add costs to close a sale? Some examples are your CRM, travel for in-person meetings, and video conferencing software. You need these figures to understand the cost of making a sale.

Step 6: Build a Sales Model

Finally, build a simple model in excel (or Google sheets) using only the existing sales team and extrapolate out for 12 months, assuming not adding any additional sales hires. Figure 3.3 is a quick snapshot example of a simple sales model.

	Month 1	Month 2	Month 3	Month 4	Month 5	Month 6	Month 7	Month 8	Month 9	Month 10	Month 11	Month 12
Sales	$128k	$120k	$109k	$130k	$117k	$102k	$97k	$111k	$121k	$142k	$113k	$122k
Days to Fully Ramp	61	68	65	13	76	16	49	22	16	15	7	12
Headcount	1	1	3	3	2	3	3	3	4	4	5	5
MRR (Monthly)	$81k	$69k	$65k	$69k	$75k	$78k	$85k	$86k	$89k	$91k	$91k	$89k
MRR/ Customer	$3k	$2k	$2k	$2k	$2k	$2k	$2k	$2k	$1k	$2k	$2k	$3k
Customers	25	24	26	29	33	34	39	40	45	46	51	36
CAC	$12k	$13k	$10k	$9k	$8k	$12k	$8k	$21k	$8k	$13k	$8k	$10k
Retention	96%	88%	96%	98%	100%	94%	100%	97%	98%	93%	96%	94%

Figure 3.3   Sales Model Example
Source: Courtesy of Austin Dressen.

Some Questions You'll Want to Be Able to Answer

How Long Does It Take until a Single Salesperson Is Cash Flow Positive?

There are several ways to actually calculate this and when your business is more mature you'll work with your finance team on what's right for the business. In the early days, I would think about it as simply the time it takes for a salesperson to generate their annual salary (or monthly salary) plus all associated costs to making a sale. This includes taxes and benefits as well as any sales tools they need. Different industries have different benchmarks for normal. *As a startup, the most important benchmark is the moment when you will run out of money before you have enough revenue to sustain your business or enough sales traction to raise outside capital.*

How Does a Salesperson's Contribution Compound over Time (Assuming No Change to the Sales Model)

Your business and business model will dictate this for you. For example, if a salesperson is selling annual subscriptions, it might take them 6 months before they are "paying for themselves." After 12 months they may be bringing in two times their costs. Assuming all customer renew their contracts, then after 18 months they are three times as profitable on a quarterly basis, and after 24 months they are four times as profitable. To be fair, it's unlikely you will have 100% customer renewal in the early days, but the point I'm trying to make is that it's important to understand how your salespeople contribute and become more profitable over time. And if they don't, it's crucial to understand why.

What Are Your Costs of Sales as a Percent of Each Sale?

Does your sale cost 10%, 50%, or 200% of the revenue generate in a single month? How does that compare to lifetime value (LTV) of a customer? For example, it could be fine that your cost of sales is greater than 100% of a single month if you have a 24-plus-month expected customer life, because your cost of sales over time will go down to a fraction of the original cost. This is a very hard metric to understand in the early days, but another one of those metrics that is fundamental to running a healthy business over time. Having a point of view that you can test and refine will both inform your sales process, product, pitch, pricing, and business model, as well as help to give future investors confidence in your thought process and understanding of the fundamentals of running a healthy and scaleable business.

What Efficiencies Can Help Improve Your Cost of Sales over Time?

1. Model in customer churn using a combination of known information, which you may not have for a while, and industry standards, which you can find on Google.
2. Start adding a couple of salespeople each quarter (into the model) and see what happens. How do sales grow? How does sale grow versus cash burn? How does it change your cost of sales? Make adjustments (along with your Financial Model) and start to build out your long-term plan.

How Do We Deal with Churn?

All companies have some level of customer churn, although the best companies have negative revenue churn. Churn is when your customers go away. The higher your churn, the stronger the signal that you are selling to the wrong customers and/or you have the wrong product. Negative churn is actually a very positive sign, and occurs when your average revenue per existing customer increases on a monthly basis. As a startup, modeling churn often seems pessimistic but in reality it's realistic. You can have the greatest salesperson in the world and be closing tons and tons of business, but if you have high churn your business will not be sustainable. Modeling churn from the beginning helps to build a culture that is not only focused on sales but also on customer satisfaction and retention. We discuss this more in Chapter 6. The key point here is to assume that some customers will churn and model that in from day one—then learn how to create negative churn.

Checking In

Check in with your plan weekly/monthly/quarterly and continue to adjust the plan frequently as you gain new information.

Chapter 4

Getting to Repeatability

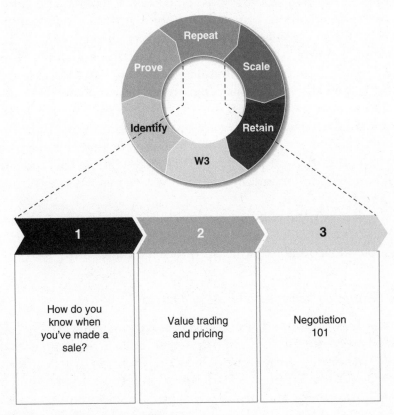

Figure 4.1 Getting to Repeatability

How Do You Know When You've Made a Sale?

By now you've identified your W3, which is to say you have a strong opinion (ideally backed up with data) on *who* your customer (ICP) is, *what* product you are selling (versus what product they are actually buying from you), and *why* they buy your product. With this framework, you've tested your theories in your customer development process by speaking with dozens (or more) of prospects, some of whom you've converted to customers. You've learned enough about your sales funnel that you've incorporated a CRM into your sales process, which has allowed you to start tracking and reporting on sales funnel metrics, and you've built out an early version of your sales model so that you can start tracking how the business is progressing. So what's next?

In this chapter, we look at the final piece needed before scaling your team so that you are prepared to hire and train the right type of salesperson for your company. More specifically, we will look at (a) value trading and pricing and (b) Negotiating 101, with the goal being an understanding of when you've made a sale (or not) (Figure 4.1).

To illustrate the challenges with knowing when you've made a sale versus when you think you've made one, I'm going to use an example of a company in my portfolio, Bamba Group.

The Difference between Interest and Intent

Bamba had developed some novel and proprietary technology that allowed them to reach rural residents in emerging markets (specifically Africa) who didn't yet own a smart phone. For many global businesses, Africa is a very important market. For many government and health agencies it is important to understand detailed information about the African populations. That said, reaching rural communities with limited wifi access and old technology is very difficult. Right now, the most common way to collect data from these communities is for people to go door-to-door asking questions. Aside from being extremely inefficient, this is also not always safe.

Bamba developed a technology along with very relevant telecom relationships that allowed the company to survey the rural population (many of whom use old flip-phones) by incentivizing them with mobile money and airtime. The way the product worked, Bamba would send out a survey to a small, targeted list in a rural community. The respondents would be incentivized with an offer of airtime to answer questions about their community, health, and other topics. At the end of the survey, the respondent would then get a message that if they shared the survey *and* the person they shared with also responded to the survey, then they would receive even more airtime. The product worked amazingly well, with the average respondent sharing the survey with over 10 more people (and the majority of those people also responding and sharing).

Bamba learned quickly that their target customer was non-government organizations (NGOs) and market research firms. They had no problem getting meetings and garnering a lot of interest. On the surface, it seemed like we had a potential rocketship on our hands. Bamba had two people selling, the CEO and a cofounder who focused on sales, and their meeting schedules were packed. We tested several different pricing structures and landed on a cost-per-completed-survey model, which fit this industry well, because they could budget for the amount of data they would collect. Furthermore, because Bamba's product worked so well, we were always able to collect more data than was required. We were also able to attract several great investors who equally got excited about these early indicators.

It looked like we were off to the races until we ran into two major challenges. First, NGOs worked on projects, meaning that they would have a specific initiative around data that they would be needing to capture. This one challenge caused two issues for Bamba: first, most of the time the NGO only knew about the project they were working on and had very little insight into what was coming up next. This made it very hard to create any repeatability and for Bamba to project sales. Second, project budgets were equivalent to raising funds for each project, which meant that even if the NGO wanted to use Bamba, they may not be the ultimate decision maker, based on approved budget.

This leads me to the second challenge, which was that while Bamba's solution was faster, safer, more accurate, and more efficient, it was considerably more expensive than sending a few local residents to go door to door. Because of this, oftentimes there was not enough budget to justify using Bamba, and likewise the cost for Bamba to operate didn't allow any additional margin for dropping the price.

In theory, we should have been able to reach product market fit. We had plenty of potential customers really excited about what we had built. Getting meetings was easy and keeping conversations live and active was also not an issue. We were solving a very real problem in a way that was faster, safer, more accurate, and more efficient, yet we were not closing a high percentage of business with this model. On the surface it looks like it was simply a matter of price, but in actuality it was about trading value (money for data). There was a value put on the data being collected that was lower than the cost of providing that data. Bamba did eventually triangulate and find their product–market fit and eventually sold their company to one of their primary customers.

* * *

There are a few lessons here and the one I want to really drive home with you is knowing when you really made a sale versus when you think you have made it. The cadence and volume of meetings early on gave Bamba and some early investors lots of confidence; however, where they ultimately fell down was in understanding the difference between interest and intent. There was lots of interest, but as we learned through the process, actual *intent* proved to be much lower, simply based on the value being traded between Bamba and their customers.

In the next couple of sections we'll dive deeper into figuring out that difference so that you can avoid the very common pitfall of "happy ears"—which is ultimately a confusion of interest and intent.

Value Trading and Pricing

Let's start with pricing. I think about pricing simply as the value you are trading with your customer. In theory it should be as simple as when you were a kid trading toys with your friends.

Your friend might have had an action figure or game that you really wanted, and vice versa. If your friend asked you to make that trade you would quickly determine how much you wanted their toy compared to the toy you were about to give up. If you wanted their toy more and, likewise, they wanted your toy more, then the trade would be made. Each one of you might feel that you were getting a better deal, and in reality you both got the best deal possible, because of the perceived value you placed on each other's toys. Selling your product to your customers should be easier than this, in that the value you bring to your customer is measurable. This means that there is a clear and quantitative way for your customer (and you) to measure the value you are trading with one another.

That being said, pricing your product can be a very daunting task. How do you know where to start? How do you know if you are capturing maximum value? What if you price it too low? What will your pricing structure look like? How will your customer measure the value they receive versus the price you are charging? How are competitive products priced and how does that align with your business model? What payment terms do you start with? What are the supporting business terms, like contract length and the ability to cancel or grow? And this is just scratching the surface!

Insights on Pricing

Before you have a full-blown panic attack, let me share with you two insights I have on early pricing:

1. *It's Better to Undercharge (versus Overcharge) Your First Customers.*

    This is actually counter to what I hear a lot of mentors say and what many founders initially think. Their belief is that you should see quickly how much you can charge so that you aren't leaving money on the table and to potentially offset more cash burn. I disagree with this theory because, while you may be successful getting customers to spend more money, ultimately if you are charging more than the value they are receiving, then you end up with an unhappy customer who will likely churn. Likewise, going back and charging less later sets up a strained relationship and potentially a lack of trust from your customers, versus raising prices later, which is common.

I'm also definitely *not* advocating that you charge nothing. Even for early pilots I believe strongly that you should charge, because you want your customer to have financial skin in the game. What I'm suggesting is that you not be afraid to start lower than where you think you'll end up. Likewise, don't get caught up in negotiating price in the early days. There are more important things you'll want to prove before you figure out your target pricing structure (such as, can you attract customers who don't cancel when their contract is done, and what is the actual value your customers receives from your product). There are plenty of opportunities to raise prices for future customers and if you are truly providing measurable value, then you'll easily be able to raise your early customer's price later, too.

2. *It Will Take You a Few Years and Many Customers Before You Can Optimize Pricing.*

Starting a company is a long-term commitment. In principle you already know this and this principle carries over to all aspects of your business, including optimizing pricing. Carrying on from the previous paragraph about undercharging, this doesn't mean you undercharge your first 100 or 1,000 customers, it means that you need to have the patience and discipline to spend time figuring out what your customers are willing to pay by understanding the true value you are trading with them. The more customers you have and the more time you have with those customers will unlock a deep understanding of the value (specifically financial impact) of your product for their company. As you learn more you can adjust price accordingly (ideally upwards). This just takes time, so be patient and pay attention.

Pricing Strategies

With that in mind, there are three ways you can think about pricing:

1. *Value-Based Pricing*

   This is a pricing strategy that sets prices primarily, but not exclusively, according to the perceived or estimated value of a product or service to the customer rather than according to the cost or product's historical prices. A good example of value-based pricing is your home internet. You likely have several package options to choose from, which range from very low and slow to lightning fast. Based on collective data from the market your internet company has priced each package based on that perceived value. When you purchase the package right for you, you do some quick calculations in your head to determine, based on the value trade of speed for money, which is the right package for you. It's unlikely you will want to pay more for a package you don't need if there is a cheaper option.

2. *Cost Plus*

   In this pricing strategy, the selling price is determined by adding a specific markup percentage to the product's unit cost. A good example of this is buying gas for your car. As you know, the price of gas changes often, as it is driven by public markets. Your local gas station buys and then prices the gasoline at a percentage above their purchase price. Because there are several gas stations in your neighborhood, they all need to price their product both as high as they can above their cost, but also low enough to be competitive with the other gas stations. When you go to buy gas, you are paying whatever price is asked, which can vary even from day to day. The value of that gas has not changed for you (you need to get to work and back), but the cost of that gas is based on what it cost the station to buy it plus the overhead needed for that station to keep its lights on and to show a profit.

3. *Wild Guessing*

This is exactly what it sounds like. While I don't really recommend this, sometimes this is just where you have to start so that you can get a baseline. This is usually the tactic you use when you have a new product in a new market and you simply don't know where to start. Inherently there are aspects of cost-plus and value-based pricing when you use this "method," but it's really just you trying to rationalize why you believe a customer will pay a certain amount. If you do find yourself needing to just guess at a starting point, my recommendation is to very quickly try to understand the value your customer is actually receiving in the trade so that you can gather enough data to move to one of the other methods.

And guess what, it doesn't really matter which pricing method you ultimately choose, because regardless of your product or company or market, the customer will never pay more (for long) than the fair value they believe they are trading. That being said, I personally always strive for value-based pricing from day one. This doesn't mean asking your prospect what they think they are willing to pay but instead involves a more intricate line of questioning so that you can determine the true value of your product for your customer, which they, in turn, validate for you.

Let me repeat that in different words: *you* need to figure out enough about your prospect's business and pain through questioning, and then provide that back to them with how your product will help make or save them money (either directly or through time/hiring) and then have them validate that value.

Pricing is tricky in established categories, exponentially more so if you are pioneering a product in a new category where your buyer may not fully appreciate the value relative to the pain you are solving. You need to prove a 10-times cost savings ROI on your product or, even better, show a direct link to revenue lift.

The challenge here is that direct attribution is very tough to prove unless you have a deep understanding of your prospect's business and how your product *directly* saves money or lifts their revenue. This requires asking probing questions about value, questions your prospect may have never considered. And that requires you to be a student of *their* business. You need to deeply understand who your customer is, what they are buying from you, and why they are buying it.

—**Rob Taylor, cofounder and CEO of Convey**

Optimizing Trade in Value and Pricing

My favorite personal example of optimizing trade in value and pricing was at BlackLocus, where after a handful of customers were onboarded, one of my team members built out a simple (but very powerful) return-on-investment (ROI) calculator. In reality it was too early for us to really understand the full-value trade we were having with our customers, but we were starting to see and collect trends around how they perceived our product to affect both top-line revenue as well as margin contribution. At this point, by using the W3 framework, we clearly identified our target customers as online retailers whose revenue was over $100 million a year and had a centralized pricing strategy with a single person being the decision maker on pricing. We also learned that for most of our customers, less than 20% of products made up greater than 80% of their revenue (and hence, where they focused their time and effort). Furthermore, in those 20% of products, our customers typically had a good understanding of how those products sold from a volume perspective and were able to project sales, revenue, and margins with decent accuracy. They became attracted to working with BlackLocus because it provided more data and transparency into the market, which turned their "decent accuracy" into high accuracy, which increased revenue and margin.

The calculator had inputs, which were assumptions on our prospect's business, as well as (data-driven) inputs on how we expected our product to impact their business, based on what we've seen with our existing customers. We'd share the calculator with our prospects (over video calls or in person), knowing that while we had some good initial data, we still had a lot to learn. We would let the prospect play around with all the inputs relative to the price we were suggesting so that they could see how their

ROI would be affected by working with us. Once the value trade was clear (and for BlackLocus it was always clearly a good value), assuming we were talking to the decision maker, we'd always get a verbal commitment in that meeting. And if we weren't talking to the right person, we now armed our contact with the information they needed to take to their boss and ultimately become a customer.

Understanding the value that is being traded between you and your customer is the ultimate key in pricing your product and maximizing the "mutual" value that both of you provide and are paid for your product—and ultimately optimizing revenue. When you are first starting out, knowing where to start will feel like a bear of a task to tackle and the stress related with "getting it right" can sometimes be overwhelming. My hope in this section is to relieve some of that stress by giving you the comfort in knowing it's okay to price low to start as well as preparing you to be okay with it taking a long time before you optimize pricing. Along the way, you'll likely get advice and even pushback on these two concepts. "You aren't charging enough or you aren't moving fast enough" is what you'll hear and you might even feel that way yourself. That's the time to step back and spend time digging into what you know and what you still have to learn about how the value is being traded between you and your customer.

Negotiation 101

In the last section we talked about pricing and value trading. The more you understand about the value being traded between you and your customer, the easier any pricing negotiation will become. This is because if you know the value you provide to your customer relative to any competitors, and your customer believes that the value they are trading is the "best deal they can get," then, assuming they actually need your product, the odds are weighted heavily in your favor that they will work with you no matter how much they try to negotiate price with you.

There have been more (great) books written about negotiating than most of us will ever read. Rather than simply repeat what others have said, my intention in this next part is to share with you my personal style of negotiation, which is: I don't.

That doesn't mean that some parts of a deal won't change and move around. In fact, it's the opposite: some parts will almost always move around (especially in a complex or enterprise sale). For me, it means that up front I set a tone of full transparency and drive the conversation around data versus emotions when talking about which points are not negotiable and which are less important.

For example, while price is a factor, it may be more important that we have a 12-month term. It may be important that we can reference the customer or it may be a requirement for the customer to meet with us monthly for feedback. Whatever the case may be, up front I always do my best to tell the prospect what points are important to me, why they are important, and where they need to be. This helps to set the stage for a very open "negotiation" process in which, rather than battling point for point on deal points, you begin to work together as a team to get the sale closed.

For example, if you know you are at your best price (which is where I always strive to start and finish), then I say up front "If this doesn't work, then we should both move on." Most people are looking for the best deal, and that is fair. Once they feel like they have the best deal (which is what you are saying) then you can focus on the rest of the deal mechanics (term, payment terms, legalese, etc.). Likewise, I also make it a point to understand, as part of the sales process, what is important for my prospect's process in the same way. Is price a factor and to what degree? Do they want any special concessions if they are an early customer? Are there payment terms they need? And, most important, how will they be measuring the success of this relationship?

I'm going to digress on that last point for just a second. In reality, how they will measure success is not likely to be an actual part of the formal deal you are making. That said, by understanding what they see as success, and how they will be measuring it will allow you to better understand the value they believe they are trading, and sets you up to make sure that you are meeting their expectations (and if you are not, this should give you the ability to get ahead of *why*, so that you can understand how to fix it).

Working Together to Reach a Deal

Early on, I spend most of my energy on making sure critical deal points are aligned and, if not, whether they can be. If a deal can't be reached, we walk away (if you are running a great sales process, you will know this long before you get to the final stages). Assuming both parties want to get the deal done, then it's simply a matter of working *together* (not as opponents) to get to a deal that everyone is happy with. I believe this is one of the most critical factors in closing sales, especially complex ones. If you and your customer negotiate as opposing players, it's much harder to work through areas of disagreement or misalignment. If you are acting as partners, then you are more apt to work together to find creative solutions for any challenging deal points.

View Your Prospect as a Partner

There are two things that I try to always do when negotiating with a prospect, or maybe better said, when working on getting a deal done. It starts with this simple visual—picture yourself and your prospect sitting on the same side of the table in a meeting. This simple visual helps to orient you to working together as a team rather than against one another. In this case, you are clearly only half the equation, but what this creates in our mind and action is the ability to approach your prospect as your partner. If you try it, what you'll notice is that your language and posture changes as you begin to work with your prospect. If you are truly visualizing yourself as being on the same side of the table and working together, it will be much easier to listen and be additive, rather than combative. If you can maintain this visualization, then your prospect will eventually match the feeling, because they will feel supported and trusted.

Take Emotion Out of the Equation

The second thing I do is to *continuously* remind myself to take any and all emotion out of the conversation. This doesn't mean you can't be high energy and enthusiastic—you should always be yourself. What it means is that I continually remind myself that this is not personal, it's business, and ultimately everyone is trying to do the best possible job. Candidly, I'm a pretty high energy and emotional person. It has literally taken me 20 years to feel like I'm mastering this, and yet I still get caught up here from time to time. It's hard because we all care so deeply about what we are doing. I will sometimes need to remind myself several times in a single conversation to curtail my emotional reactions and stick to the data to get the deal done—which often means letting your ego go.

I've negotiated hundreds (if not thousands) of things in my life and as I've become more competent at staying level-headed and data driven, I've seen a direct correlation with accomplishing more successful deals (or knowing much sooner when to walk away). Maybe more important, it's allowed me to control the conversation in terms of always getting to truth. The most extreme example of this is when I'm negotiating with a relatively irrational person who is also emotionally driven. Sometimes that is a deliberate negotiating tactic and sometimes it's just that person's personality. In either case, they are looking to create an emotional argument, either because they don't have the data or don't understand the data to make a good decision. When I don't match their emotion, keep it data driven, and spend time trying to understand the motivation behind their reaction, it gives me the ability to listen and see if we can get to the root of what they really want to accomplish.

I want you to keep in mind that some deals just won't get done, because the value being traded between you and your customer doesn't seem fair to one of you. The key to getting any deal done is understanding what your prospect (really) needs and making sure you are clear on what is important to you. Keeping your own emotions in check greatly increases your chances of that deeper understanding and ultimately making a sale.

The Process of Making a Deal

So how does this manifest into actually working with your prospect and making a sale?

Start with a Conversation

First and foremost, and I cannot stress this enough, *never* negotiate over email. Email should be used for setting up meetings, clarifying points, recapping meetings, and sending documents. Email should never, ever be used for closing a sale. In this section we're focused on negotiating, which starts with the proposal. Always get on the phone or arrange a video call and walk your prospect through the proposal. Explain points that you think are important or that could be complicated. Let them ask questions and have a conversation. Then and only then should you send a proposal over. And the same goes for any major (and ideally minor) point you are negotiating around.

There are a couple of ways in which I try to always accomplish this. The first is that, whenever possible (and realistic due to finances, cost of the product, etc.) I try to have the big conversations in person. Not only do I try to do them in person, but I request that we meet in a small meeting room where we can sit next to each other (*not* across the table from each other). Remember what I said before about visualizing working next to each other at a table; well, this is your chance to use that visualization, and when you are both in that small room, it's likely that your prospect will be in a similar mindset. Sometimes this is hard to coordinate, especially when you travel to them. I will typically try to let my prospect sit first and then say, "Hey, I'm going to sit next to you so that we can work on this together more easily." Very few people will reject this idea, and if you do it casually and sincerely enough it won't be awkward but instead it will set the tone for collaborating as a team.

Often meeting in person isn't an option. My next go-to is always a video call. While technically you are still sitting "across" from each other, you are able to see one another, which helps to gauge intent and emotion, and makes the meeting into a conversation between two real people.

Having these conversations over the phone is always my third option and is still preferable to email. Since talking on the phone can lack a personal feel, it becomes even more important to continually visualize yourself sitting next to each other at a table, and likewise to continuously remind yourself to leave the emotion out of the conversation. Even though I always strive for in-person or video calls, I'd guess that better than 50% of my negotiations still happen over the phone. Even if my contact emails me, unless it's something we are simply agreeing to, I'll pick up the phone and call them in return. In my experience, a five-minute phone call can almost always get you to truth faster and with much less drama.

Be Truthful and Transparent

Whenever I'm "negotiating" or working with a prospect to get a deal for the first time, they are always a bit thrown off, confused at first, and sometimes maybe even a tiny bit frustrated. This is because most people think about negotiating as going over deal points in detail, point for point, and specifying prices and terms. In my experience very few people, much less salespeople, negotiate by not negotiating. Typically each side will posture a bit or will hold some information back. They will usually also assume that the other person is doing the same. They will assume that you have wiggle room and that you are trying to take advantage of them—this is why you often hear people say "I hate salespeople." Guess what, I hate those types of salespeople, too, which is why I've worked very hard over the past 25 years to always be truthful and transparent. Because of this, I feel like I've been very successful in closing the most important sales in a way where everyone feels like each side got the best deal they could get. This strategy has always helped in getting a sale closed because my prospect quickly learns that I'm honest and working with them (not against them) to create the fairest trade possible for all parties.

I also realize this style doesn't work for everyone, but if you are going to try it, the most important thing to remember is that everything you say must be 100% fully transparent. If you can build that honesty muscle, you will find that every deal, which should close will. Likewise, deals that ultimately shouldn't be closed, won't be closed. This is a good thing, because when you close the wrong customers you end up spending more time with unhappy people and ultimately will have churn.

Knowing When the Deal Is Ready to Close

The final point I'll touch on in this part is "How will I know when the sale is done?"

First off, and to be very clear, you have not closed a sale until a written agreement has been signed. This means that all business and legal points have been agreed upon. This includes price, term of the agreement, and payment terms. Not only is it very clear how long your customer will be paying you, what the amount is, and when, but there will be legal paperwork (contract, agreement, purchase order) that you both have signed. This makes the agreement legally binding and official. Until that point, any deal can fall through, regardless of intent. You should not celebrate until both contracts are signed (and ideally money is in the bank).

That being said, there are a few clear indicators when those two things are most likely going to happen. The caution here is to beware of "happy ears." This is when you think your prospect is ready to buy because you are an optimistic entrepreneur or salesperson and think you are hearing all the right signals.

To avoid happy ears, let's go back to your sales process and the negotiations. You can create a checklist of the items you've learned along the way that says, as you go from stage to stage, that certain things need to happen. Put this list in your CRM. For example, do you have verbal acknowledgment from the actual decision maker who can approve the budget? Have you already agreed on a price, term, and payment terms? Do you have a start date and onboarding plan in place? If there is a technical implementation, is that team on board and knows that this is coming? If you are selling to enterprise companies, you may also have to go through a procurement process. We won't cover procurement in this book, but if you aren't familiar, procurement is a separate division of an enterprise company whose entire job is to make sure that before any money gets spent, there is a "second set of eyes" to go over the deal and legal points. Procurement can be a beast and will often kill deals. It's not uncommon for you and your contact to be in full agreement and then for procurement to come in and try to renegotiate everything. In these cases it's even more important for you and your contact to be in full agreement about the relationship, so that your contact can (and should) be working with you to get through procurement. If you are ever selling to enterprises, one of your first questions should be about their procurement process, so that you can start preparing early.

If any box is not checked, then that is a weakness in your ability to close the sale, and when all the boxes are checked, then you will know that 90% of the time (or even more, barring an act of nature), your sale will close. Similar to your sales process, early on you just have to make an educated guess on this checklist. Over time, you should be revisiting that checklist and comparing it to your data to refine it. Once you are in scale mode, you should have greater than 95% confidence in that being the final checklist, so that your sales team can just go through their process, check off the items that get them closer to closing each deal, and ultimately close the sale.

Chapter 5

Scaling Your Team for Speed

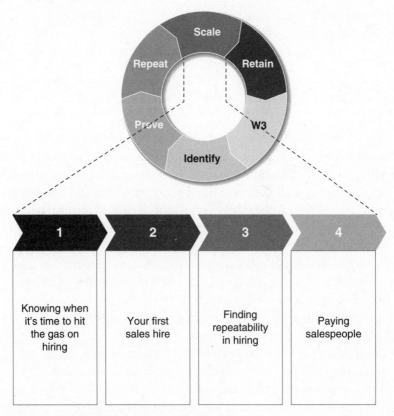

Figure 5.1 Scaling Your Team for Speed

Knowing When It's Time to Hit the Gas on Hiring

I look for PPC, the three things that signal a tech startup is at the first tipping point in its life cycle and likely able to successfully scale-up sales. First P is Product, *broadly the product–market fit*

107

is established and product execution is a solid B, without which sales beyond innovators and early adopters won't happen soon.

Second P is People, *specifically the team's readiness to learn and grow into the coming tipping points of revenue growth, which really means abandoning what worked well for sales in the previous tipping point (i.e. MVP).*

C is for a critical mass of customers *evidenced by 10+ lighthouse customers—these are customers who sing praises about your solution addressing their pain points, unequivocal evidence that Product and People have matured sufficiently to scale up sales.*

—David Loia, CRO at ScaleFactor

Up to this point, we've spent our time focused on building our foundation so we are poised to sell more faster. We've used the W3 framework from Chapter 1 to identify *who* our customer is, *what* they are buying, and *why* they need your product. In Chapter 2 we learned the difference between customer development and sales and how to use the customer development process to identify our ideal customer profile (ICP). In Chapter 3 we took the data and information from Chapter 2 to identify our sales process, and set up systems to track and measure (CRM) the sales cycle as well as use that data to develop some early models. And in Chapter 4 we looked at how to price our products, negotiate with our customers, and close more business.

At this point you are probably feeling pretty good, as you should. You have some customers and some revenue. You are feeling some confidence around product–market fit and everyone involved in your company (employees and investors) are getting hyped up on your initial traction. Now is the time to build your sales team and start scaling revenue.

On the surface this sounds easy. I mean, you are able to sell your product to pretty much any perspective buyer, so any good salesperson should be able to as well, right? Well, maybe, but it's not that easy.

Building out and scaling your sales organization can be very tricky and can kill your company if you do it wrong. But do it right and you will see your sales and revenue skyrocket. The reason it's tricky is because it's not as simple as posting an ad for a salesperson. There are many things to consider. How much sales experience do your salespeople need? How much industry knowledge is necessary to be successful? Do you want people who have industry contacts? What personality types fit the company culture you are building and what is the sales culture you hope to build? These are just a few of the many questions you'll be answering—even if you don't know all the questions yet. Those first few sales hires are not only crucial to growing your customer base and generating revenue, they will also play a big part in your company culture.

And for this reason, hiring salespeople, especially the first few, is a different kind of hard than hiring developers or product people or finance people. Those roles tend to be more specific skill sets that you can test against, whereas salespeople come in all shapes and sizes. So much about a person's ability to be a successful salesperson is about their personality on top of their product and industry knowledge and in addition to their ability to sell. Also, your salespeople are the face of your company.

> I look for someone who can clearly articulate past performance and success in the role, first and foremost. Not generalized statements, which you'll find happen a lot (e.g. I brought in $1 million in new business in my last year) but specifics: "I closed 35 customers totaling $1.2 million in new business, hit quota every quarter I was at the company, was the top rep eight out of my nine quarters, etc." This shows they craft a plan and play to *win*. A winning culture on a sales team is energizing and infectious to others. On the sales floor, it takes that one bell to ring to get it ringing more and more!
>
> I also interview for curiosity and the ability to ask great questions, which shows a desire to learn from others and to get at the heart of what really matters. This is not crucial in

sales, but as a member of a great team and culture, I look to see if they can challenge my thinking in a respectful way, while taking direction and feedback, if they are someone who seeks to understand the vision and align themselves to it.

And finally, the most important piece: hard-working, commonsensical people. When it gets tough, individually and amongst the team, you need someone who will work harder than the next person, for themselves and others, solving problems no matter what. I've found common sense isn't very common. Without it, people tend to make things matter that don't, strive for the wrong things, and prove to be more confusing and a bit of a cultural distraction.

——**Autumn Manning, founding CEO of YouEarnedIt**

In this chapter we will cover three things (Figure 5.1). In the following section, we will discuss how to hire your *first* salesperson. We'll talk about timing, attributes, expectations, and how to know when they are the right or wrong hire. In the "Finding Repeatability in Hiring" section, we will dive into your next hires, as well as how and when to scale. And finally in the "Paying Salespeople" section, we will dive into compensation.

Your First Sales Hire

Salesperson effectiveness, more than any other role, is company stage and type dependent. It is hard to get right and easy to get wrong at the early stages of refining product–market fit, as your first sales hire must both help to refine fit and sell the product in the process. In the early days, you are not repeatedly selling a widget, you are selling a solution, testing various messages across several possible buyers in order to find the best combination of pain description that fits with your solution.

It is a special skill that requires a deeply experienced, early-stage seller who can point to multiple successes finding fit and getting to $5 million in revenue run rate. My approach has always been to find a player/coach for this first role who can step in and do the work initially, then build the early team. The first

hire is not about solving for the long term, it is about finding
that unique individual who gives you the best chance of figuring
out market fit and getting to initial repeatability in your selling
motion.
                    —Rob Taylor, cofounder and CEO of Convey

It would be great if it were as easy as just hiring some
salespeople … but it's not. The process of figuring out the right
profile, how to get them trained and set up for success, and
figuring out the right compensation structure takes time and
some patience (from both you and the people you hire).

After hiring well over 100 people and interviewing probably
close to 1,000 I've developed a process that has worked well
for me. First, you need to have more than a single customer;
depending on your business, sales process, and cycle it could be
as few as three to four or as many as more than 20. The thing to
clue in on here is not the number of customers but the data (and
comfort in that data) of your understanding in everything we've
already discussed. More specifically, do you know your W3? Can
you clearly articulate and support with data *who* your customer is,
what they are buying, and *why* they need your product? Have you
gone through the customer development process to validate that
you know your ICP and have some product–market direction?
If you do not have high confidence with data to support it,
then you are not ready to hire your first salesperson. I don't
care what your peers or investors tell you, I promise that until
you have a high degree of confidence here you will set up your
first sales hire to fail, setting you back and making you sell
less slower.

I do want to point out an important distinction here. In
Chapter 3 we discuss the difference between customer development and sales. There are a few people who are actually very
good at doing customer development, and there are cases where
you'll want to hire such a person to help you figure out your W3;
just keep in mind that this means extra headcount before you've
proven there is a business to support the hire. That being said,
if you are a technical CEO and also responsible for building the
product, a great customer development counterpart (cofounder
or early hire) may be necessary.

While I think it's important to read this chapter now so that you know what to expect and the signals to look for, I'd suggest coming back to this chapter once you feel like you are getting close to nailing your W3.

So you are now ready to start hiring salespeople, awesome! I'm sure you are pumped because you can already see the money flowing in and a path to hundreds of millions of dollars in revenue! Before you go out and hire a team of salespeople, you still have some more work and validation to do. And to get started go hire ONLY ONE person. Why one? Well as the founder and/or CEO you will likely be better at selling your product than anyone (at least initially).

We have a few goals with this first hire, and also the second and third, which is to see if anyone else can sell your product, what type of salespeople you should hire, what kind of team structure is needed, what kind of support salespeople will need, and what you want the sales culture to be. In this chapter my goal is to give you some foundational framework and shorthand to get you started.

Thinking about hiring this first person can be another one of those daunting tasks, which is why I see so many founders punt on the hard work of figuring out who the right person is for their business and just look for really strong sellers, assuming the rest will fall into place. If you are lucky, they will, but there are so many different types of people and personalities out there that the odds are not in your favor. For thinking about the first hire, I've developed a list of attributes that I look for. And I try to be very disciplined in this first hire and not compromise very much—the cost of getting it wrong is just too high.

These are the five attributes I look for in my first hires and what I encourage all my founders to do. For me, this is the priority order I think about when evaluating potential hires.

Attribute 1: Experience Selling at an Early Stage Company, Typically in the First Five Hires

I really can't stress this enough: many people are attracted to working at a startup. They see stories or have friends who have made a ton of money in salary and equity. They hear the stories of ping-pong tables, paid lunches, and unlimited perks. As we know, the reality of working at a startup, especially in the early days, is the exact opposite. The pay sucks, risk is high, and your office is small, cramped, and old, if you have an office at all. There isn't anyone to create your sales presentation or take out the trash, it's all on you. If someone hasn't been through that experience before (or longs to do it again) it's a nonstarter for me in almost any case.

When you do find that person, really dig in on what their experience was like. Do they paint a picture that it was hard and scary and they both loved it and thrived at it? Or do they paint a rosy picture? Do they complain and make excuses for why it didn't go well, or if it did, how do they talk about their contribution? I'd love to tell you that there are quantitative data points you can pull out here, but frankly there are not. You need to get a sense whether this person really did work in an early stage environment where there were tons of unknowns, lots of risk, and they loved it and thrived. Listen to your gut, regardless of what their resume says. If your gut feels good, then check that box; if not, pass and move on.

Attribute 2: Tenure in That Company to a Much Larger Team/Higher Revenue (for Example, 5 to 50 Salespeople and/or $100 000 to $10 Million or More in Revenue)

The reason this is important is because, for me, it shows 4 things: resilience, dedication, loyalty, and an understanding of how the startup world works. This doesn't mean that you may not find someone awesome who hasn't seen a full cycle like this, but what we're trying to do here is hedge our risk. Hiring is hard; finding great people who can last is even harder. And when you can use little data points like this to help give you confidence that it's a strong hire, use them.

When interviewing candidates and talking about their history, specifically tenure in an early stage company, really dig in on what *their* experience was like through the growth. Again, you are looking for people who relish and thrive on growing pains, look back at their time with pride, and want to go through all that pain again. Also dig into what their contribution was throughout the growth.

This will tell you a lot about what kind of employee they will be for you. Did they continue to grow within the organization, get promoted, and take on more responsibility, or did they stay a seller?

There actually isn't a wrong answer here; however, it's important to know these things so that you can determine what kind of contributor they will be for you. If you want someone who will grow and take on more responsibility, and you are talking to someone who was a top seller for five years but now wants to move into management, take some time to figure out why they weren't promoted in their last gig. There could be lots of reasons, and good ones, but typically in an early-stage company, exceptional people will take on more responsibility over time. This person may be a phenomenal seller but if they are not able to take on more responsibility and you need them to, then it's not a fit. If you and they are okay with taking a sales role that will likely always be a sales role, then you may have found a great fit for your company.

Attribute 3: Self-Motivation and Ability to Persevere through Tough Times (This Doesn't Have to Be in Business, It's a Life Attribute)

Even though this is third on the list, in many ways I consider this the most important attribute of any startup hire. I've worked in and with startups for over 20 years and there is only one guarantee: this shit is hard! There will be so many ups and downs. It will feel dire on more than one occasion. You'll be close to running out of money, or people won't be buying your product, or they will be unhappy or you'll have made a bad hire that is hurting morale, or a cofounder will leave or not be holding their weight. The point here is that you need to find mentally tough people who can not only work through the hard times but can be collaborative and creative and take initiative.

It's great when you find someone who's been through some tough times in business and can articulate what they went through, how they persevered, and it's even better if they smile and tell the story with joy. I like to ask them what they learned, what could have been done differently, and how they would approach the same situation(s) now that they have experience.

The answers here can be very revealing. For example, do they take responsibility or blame others? Are they thoughtful in describing what they learned and how they would approach things today in detail, or do they talk about it with less understanding of what could have been handled differently? Spending time understanding how this person truly behaves in hard times is important and also difficult to uncover in the interview process. The closest thing I've found to figure this out is try to get into some kind of negotiation with them before you make an offer, it can even be in discussion of what compensation would look like. How do they handle themselves? While not perfect, this is a bit of an indication of how they will fare when times get tough.

I also like to look at other aspects of their life. What are their hobbies and what do they do in their free time? Do they challenge themselves constantly or do they spend their free time doing more relaxing hobbies? I personally love working with athletes, and I don't just mean that they were athletes in the past. It's great if you played a college sport and were good at it—but do you still play something? The reason I like athletes is because, in order to stay competitive as you get older, have a job, and maybe even start a family, the discipline you need to stay competitive and fit is quite difficult, but it's a behavior that typically carries across anything that person does in his or her life. Additionally, anyone who has played any sport for long enough has won, lost, been injured, come back from injury, and in general has been through all kinds of emotions and kept going.

This doesn't mean that there aren't awesome people who are not athletic, this is simply an attribute I've identified as an indicator of a good salesperson. It's personal and you will find those indicators for yourself in time as well.

Attribute 4: Long-Term (versus Short-Term) Financially Motivated

This is important because, as a startup, you'll pay them less. Base salary will likely be below market, commissions will be lower at first, and they'll need to understand and value equity. This is a tough one to tease out. Most people applying to a startup will be somewhat familiar with the lower pay and equity components but that doesn't mean that they really understand the financial implications in the short term and it also doesn't mean they really have the capacity to take on that risk.

Assuming they've been through this before, that would give me much more confidence that they at least understand what they are getting into, but people's lives change.

If they haven't been through this before, you have a real responsibility to drive a candid conversation about the reality of what they are getting into.

Startups are risky and everyone has a different level of risk tolerance. At the same time, there is no "right" or "wrong" time; the important thing is that everyone goes in with aligned expectations and eyes wide open about the risk involved. People come into startups from all types of backgrounds and at all points. I know an incredible CEO who raised her seed round while six months pregnant; it was hard, but she had great support and knew what she was getting into. I also know another founder who realized he needed to step back and find a more stable role to be able to know he'd support his family and pay his mortgage.

The key here isn't to find out someone's financial situation or home life and make a judgment about whether they are ready for this; in fact from an HR perspective you can't legally ask many of these questions anyway.

The point here is to have a really candid conversation around short- versus long-term financial expectations, appetite for risk, and a personal runway to join you. These questions are all fair game and really important for both of you to have level, set expectations before you hire that person.

Attribute 5: Has a Track Record of Working with Lots of Autonomy While Also Having a Strong Grounding in Personal Accountability

When your company is young and there aren't many employees, everyone has to wear multiple hats. A byproduct of having to wear many hats and having limited resources is that often even the best managers don't have time to be good managers. Because of this, early on you need to be hiring people who don't need to be managed. In fact, more so than needing to be managed, your first hires (not just sales hires) need to have a deep understanding of what needs to happen to move the business forward, and how to prioritize the 10,000 things happening at once and take ownership regardless of if things go well or not. This doesn't mean that you don't provide direction, what it means is that once your salesperson has direction and you believe you are aligned, they are able to overcome new hurdles as well as grow new opportunities with little hands-on management by you. That doesn't mean they are calling the shots and don't need to get your approval for major items; what it means, stated very simply, is that they know what their job is and they get it done.

You may be able to find someone who has all the first four attributes, but if that person requires ongoing hands-on management and direction it can take too much of your time. This isn't a nonstarter for me but given the choice between someone who can clearly work autonomously and someone who requires more management, especially for that first sales hire, I'll always opt for the person who can work on their own. And there is another benefit to this, which is that the person who doesn't need to be heavily managed has some ability to be strategic and collaborate with you as you think about growing the sales team and the business, because inherently in that skill set is the ability to see the bigger picture.

The caution here is that there are people who work incredibly well with autonomy but aren't great at having personal accountability. This can be devastating because on the surface you think you are working with exactly the right person, but when things start going wrong, and they always do, the person who doesn't understand accountability will start to lay blame on everyone else rather than taking on the initiative to help the company grow and get better.

How Will I Know When Someone Has Any of These Five Traits?

These traits are a little easier to tease out during an interview. The way I go about it is to ask them how they worked with their previous manager, what their communication was like, and how they tackled challenges together. If the person tells you something like their manager gave them direction and checked in regularly but was pretty hands-off, that's a good start. If they describe challenging situations in a way that gives you the sense that they took ownership by fixing the challenge or soliciting the right help, that's even better. Conversely if they reported to their manager and their manager didn't give them the ability or autonomy to try and fix challenges on their own, that could be a negative signal. You do have to be careful here, though, because it just as easily could be a manager issue, though I've found the best employees can gain the trust of any manager and are open to accepting responsibility.

Take your time with this first hire—do not rush. This hire is crucial to get right, otherwise you'll need to start this process over, meaning you'll lose time and revenue and put the success of your business at risk, no matter how awesome your product is. Get to know this person in an office setting and outside. Develop confidence both in their ability to do a great job and also to be adaptive to your company culture (salespeople tend to be loud and outgoing and early salespeople can play a big part in shaping culture, so be really diligent here). Make sure you get along. You don't necessarily need to be making a lifelong friend but they should be someone you think you can trust and can see spending a lot of time with. I have a mental test I do with all potential hires, which I call "the airport test": I ask myself whether, if I were walking in an airport in a strange city and saw them but they didn't see me, I would walk over to them to make small talk. If the answer is, "I don't know" or "no," then pause and figure out why. Even if they are exceptional, this first hire is someone you'll be spending a lot of time with and if you already aren't sure you'd want to spend time with them, you probably won't. This is a bit less important for future hires, but for this first one ask yourself if they pass the airport test.

> As a recruiter who has worked with some of the best startups in Austin, I have to caution you … hiring the right salesperson to help jump-start your company is vital and will determine whether or not you will be around this time next year.
>
> You need someone who can produce amidst a lot of ambiguity! A salesperson who can function without processes, defined marketing strategy, and someone that can hunt as well as they close.

Look for a seasoned salesperson from the startup world, who has experience taking a new product/service to market. Someone who is not afraid, who is passionate about the company and money driven!

If they don't have any of the above qualities, or even if they hit 75%, they are not the right salesperson to launch your company.

Reference check back channels!

Take your time selecting your first sales rep … they will be the face of your company. They are the first contact the money holder has with your brand … this isn't something you want to rush!

—**Kalyn Blacklock, senior talent acquisition manager at Convey**

What Do I Do Once I Think I Found My First Sales Hire?

Once you find the person, but before they start, put together a really loose training plan. And write it down. Take the time to make sure their first week has some structure to it. Great salespeople will want to jump right on the phone, so make sure they have the information they need to make good decisions when they start reaching out to potential customers. In your plan, make sure you describe to them the process you've been through (all the preceding chapters in this book) and what you've learned. Show them not only what they should do but why. Early on I don't spend a ton of time creating materials and rigid structure; instead I like to spend time helping tell the "sales process story." Arm your salesperson with knowledge and the basic tools discussed in Chapter 3 and then quickly get out of their way, *but* make sure they know you are there to help, support, and ensure their success.

I strongly suggest that out of the gate you set a precedence with some sort of regular meeting cadence; at bare minimum, plan a weekly one-on-one and be extremely disciplined with attendance. Initially I'd set up an hour's meeting but as you get into a good rhythm you can likely change to 30 minutes. Depending on your team size, company culture, and how everyone works together, you may also have another weekly meeting with all stakeholders, including the salesperson.

In your one-on-one meeting you want to talk about pipeline and progress and, especially early on, at least half the meeting should focus on the learning process, how it's different from what was expected as well as recommendations for optimizing that learnings (which could fall on anyone, including the salesperson). This could be anything from the sales process to your ICP to the product or messaging. It's very important to be going through this process with your first hire before you bring any other salespeople into the company because essentially what you are doing is moving one step closer to creating a repeatable sales process, which means that you know, with a high degree of confidence, all the elements of how to grow sales (people, product, customers, etc.). When you have a repeatable sales process you are ready to scale and take off like a rocket, and until that point you simply need to put all the pieces in place. By working with this first hire closely to confirm all that you've learned and refine your understanding, you are collecting more data, which is getting you one big step closer.

Within 60 days (if not sooner) you will have a good sense of whether this is a great hire or a miss. You'll be able to tell not only by the meetings they are setting up but how those meetings are progressing and the feedback you are getting from them and potential customers. You'll also have a good sense of how they will fit into the culture you are trying to build. My hope for you is that you feel great after 45 or so days, but if the jury is still out at 60 days, my experience says the jury will never conclude, so cut your losses and start over.

Once you are sure that this is a great hire (but not sooner than 60 days), take a look at the newly collected data (you now have two people selling, you and your salesperson) and re-evaluate everything from your W3 to your process and funnel metrics and maybe even compensation. There are almost certainly some adjustments to be made based on new learnings. Figure out what those things are, make them, and then get ready to hire your next few salespeople.

Finding Repeatability in Hiring

When hiring for salespeople at my first startup, Pinpoint Technologies, I used to struggle on whether it was more important to hire for sales experience or for industry experience. Our product was dispatch software for ambulances, so the features were pretty nuanced. Potential customers were using the software to save lives, so they asked detailed questions, full of industry jargon—how do you handle SSM plans, where do you store post locations, what about prescheduled transports, etcetera.

One of my cofounders was our first VP of sales and he was the rare unicorn—a natural sales guy with deep industry experience. His sales technique was to say "name a situation—I'll show you how the software can handle it." He was very successful, so when we made early sales hires, we looked for people who could do the same, and that required industry experience. But guess what? They couldn't close!

Eventually, we came to learn that the best approach was to hire for sales experience and to use a different technique. Instead of the "ask me anything, I dare you!" sales approach, we began to hire experienced salespeople and gave them a script and a sales engineer. It was a game changer!

—David Brown, co-CEO, Techstars

Once you make the adjustments you learned in the "Your First Sales Hire" section, you are ready to hire the next two to three (max) salespeople. There are two things you are trying to learn here which are meant to help you figure out how to find repeatability in hiring salespeople and to hire more great people faster. But before you can get there, we need to learn how.

Validating That Multiple People Can Sell Your Product

The first thing you are trying to learn and confirm is whether more than the two of you can sell your product, and what are the unique attributes your future salespeople need in order to be successful. This is similar to when you hired your first person. You had some early success yourself acquiring new customers, but you are special. As a founder, you have more skin in the game, more enthusiasm, and more knowledge than just about anyone. And as we talked about in the preceding section, in most cases you are the best salesperson for a long time. Just as with your first hire and getting validation that it's not just a founder who can sell, with your next few hires we are seeking similar validation. Is this a product anyone can sell or are you and your first salesperson special? What are the unique attributes of your product and company that will help determine who you should be hiring? These could be things like industry knowledge, company culture, customer type (enterprise or midmarket or SMB), or sale type. Likewise, what do you believe are the unique attributes of the people you will hire? How much experience will they need? Do they need enterprise or SMB experience? Do they need any sort of formal sales training or industry training and how will they fit into your culture?

At the point when you decide to hire your next few salespeople, you will have strong opinions on all of these things. Write them all down. Work with your first sales hire to see if they agree. Once you make the hires you will want to go back and validate your assumptions and note changes before you go on to the next set of hires and start scaling.

Hiring at a Faster Pace and Training

The other thing you are trying to learn is how to hire at a faster pace. While hiring begins by validating that more than just two people can sell your product and by understanding the attributes needed to be successful, that's only the first part. Once you have this validation you then need to figure out how to put it into practice. You will need to figure out how to find people with similar attributes to the ones you've identified. Are there specific companies or company types where you can find them? Do they have a specific training in common? Are there personality types that would enable your salespeople to be more successful.

The other part of this is training. Now that you've hired one person and validated more assumptions, you'll want to put a more specific training plan (see Figure 5.2) in place for your next group of hires. My recommendation is to start outlining what your training plan will look like at the same time that you start writing job descriptions. You won't need to go into detail yet, but these are the methods, which will inform each other. As you think about what type of salesperson you are hiring and what attributes are important, you can also be thinking about what kind of training plan will be necessary for your salespeople to be successful. For example if

New Hire Training Plan — Company Mobile

Monday	Topic	With
9:30–10:30 am	Orientation, Training Plan Overview	
10:30–11:00 am	Sales Team and Commission Plan Overview	Sales Team Member
11:00–12:00 pm	Delivery Overview	Sales Team Member
12:00–1:00 pm	Welcome Lunch	Sales Team
1:30–2:30 pm	Competitor Training	Sales Manager
2:30–5:00 pm	Self-Review – Industry Research	Self

Tuesday		
10:30–11:30 am	Client Service/Strategic Accounts Demo/Overview	Sales Team Member
11:30–12:00 pm	Self-Review	Self
12:00–1:00 pm	Lunch Break	
2:00–3:00 pm	Company Mobile Sales Process	Sales Team Member
3:00–4:00 pm	SFDC Training on Company Mobile's Process	Sales Team Member
4:00–5:00 pm	Watch Sales Demo/Calls	Sales Team Member

Wednesday		
10:00–11:00 am	Prospecting	Sales Team Member
11:00–11:30 am	CEO Session	CEO
1:00–2:00 pm	Watch Sales Demo/Calls	Sales Member
2:00–3:00 pm	Watch Sales Demo/Calls	Sales Member
3:00–4:00 pm	Weekly Sales Meeting	Sales Manager
4:30–5:00 pm	Self-Review – Company Mobile platform and Pitch	Self

Thursday		
9:00–11:30 am	Self-Review	Self
11:30–12:30 pm	Weekly Sales/Client Success Meeting	All Sales and C/S
2:00–2:30 pm	Technology Overview	
3:00–4:00 pm	Pricing and Proposals	Sales Manager
4:00–5:00 pm	Role Playing	

Friday		
9:00–12:00 pm	Get on the Phones	Self
2:00–5:00 pm	Prospecting and Prepping for Next Week	Self
5:30 pm	Company Social Event	All

Figure 5.2 New Hire Training Plan

your product is highly technical, you will need to determine how much time to spend training on the product. If your product is less technical and you are hiring industry experts, then you may need much less time on the product and more time on the process and pitch. It's impossible to inform you in this book what kind of training plan you'll want to put in place for your new sales hires, however, Figure 5.2 shows an example of a one-week training plan for a SaaS company that sells analytic software to developers.

An important note: Your first salesperson should be involved in both the hiring process and the training process. They should be interviewing every candidate and spending extra time with finalists, and they should be on board with your choices (even if they don't fully agree). This draws your salesperson into helping them succeed and build the company. Then when it comes time to build out a training plan, ask your salesperson what you could have done better and for recommendations on how to bring this team on. This both gives your salesperson more ownership in their success and also puts your salesperson in teaching mode, which forces them to deeply understand the process and cycle and customers. Finally, you should share your adjusted model and expectations of the new hires with your salesperson and do a gut check about goals. You may both be wrong, but at least then you've done a solid check-in before they start. And you should expect that you are wrong about many of your assumptions—and that's okay. You're about to add a whole new dimension into your company and process which will turn everything upside down—this is what we want!

> Here's the reality, you will probably get your first sales hire wrong, given how hard it is to get right. Internalize this reality and use it to ensure a disciplined approach to hiring your first sales player/coach. Compromising on criteria for this first hire can result in wrong messaging to wrong buyer, suboptimal pricing, and, most important, lost time and burning more cash. But the most insidious side effect of the wrong first hire? Finding some early traction that leads you down a dead end because the selling process wasn't broad enough in its exploration and discovery.
> **—Rob Taylor, cofounder and CEO of Convey**

Your next hires should all start on the same day as a peer group. They should both learn from each other and be competitive with one another. None of them should feel they have an advantage or disadvantage relative to *your* company. This group should have many if not all of the same attributes as your first hire. Once they have started and are all trained, let them get to work.

Diversity Is a Must-Have

One thing I strongly encourage as you add this next group of hires is to look for diversity, all kinds of diversity. Personality, background, race, ethnicity, gender, and any other type of diversity you can find. There are, at least, two important benefits to this. The first is that you have a wider pool of data to help identify the best attributes of your sales team versus hiring carbon copies of yourself. Obviously *you* are awesome, and we would clone you if we could, but since that's not possible, the next best choice is to widen your net. While ultimately you are looking for a personality archetype, you still won't have enough data to exactly know what that is. The second benefit is that, at an early stage you start to build a diverse workforce. Again, there could be several books written simply about how diversity in the workplace drives better outcomes and every study I've ever read confirms this. Equally as important, you are inherently encouraging a culture of collaboration, creativity, and openness.

I asked Jason Thompson, VP of diversity and inclusion at Techstars, for his advice:

> Research shows that diverse teams have better outcomes, so let's start with diverse teams! It is never too soon to think about success or how to build a successful team. Recruiting a diverse team is part of that process. A recent study by Morgan Stanley showed more diverse companies had better returns and were less volatile. Diverse teams help your bottom line.
>
> In order to build a diverse team faster, I recommend following these simple steps:
>
> 1. Identify a D&I leader
> 2. Collect data
> 3. Check your bias
> 4. Network to recruit
> 5. Interview four
>
> [Here is an explanation of those steps.]
>
> 1. *Identify a Leader*
>   Identify someone to focus on diversity. In larger companies, this can be a chief diversity officer; in a small company, it can be you. Everyone in the company can and should be committed to diversity, but at the

end of the day someone has to do the work. I have seen a lot of D&I programs and initiatives fail because everyone agrees to diversity and inclusion, but no one is responsible to get it done.

2. *Collect D&I Data*

I recommend you start with a simple definition of how you define diverse employees. Typically, this is individuals who are underrepresented in your industry. This would include people of color, persons with disabilities, gender, gender identity, LGBTQ, and others.

After you define diversity, compile the data on the percentage of underrepresented groups in your company, industry, and specific job title you are recruiting to fill. This gives you the baseline. Now you know where you started and can measure your success against this metric.

3. *Check Your Bias*

There are a lot of bias trainings and some online assessments you can take to learn about bias. A very popular one is Project Implicit (https://implicit.harvard.edu/implicit/index.jsp). I strongly suggest you learn about your bias, but there is a simple bias test I can give you right now.

If when thinking about recruiting diverse candidates your first response is: "We want qualified candidates" or "We can't lower our standards," then this reflects bias. Focusing on recruiting candidates that are underrepresented does not mean "lowering your standards" or "less qualified." If you automatically thought "less qualified" or "lower standards" it reflects your bias. You need to do some honest self-assessment about your thinking when it comes to women, people of color, people with disabilities, LGBTQ, and other identities.

4. *Network to Recruit*

You have probably already done quite a bit of recruiting from your personal network to find and recruit talent. Now you need to be intentional. Let individuals in your network know diversity is important to your company, and let them know you want to identify and recruit diverse talent.

Recruit within your network and outside of your network to find great candidates. If you have identified a person to lead your D&I work, they can begin building a simple list of events to attend to grow your network. If you are a small company with a limited budget, contact regional colleges and universities. (Don't assume you can only recruit at historically black colleges and universities.) Most have someone to lead their diversity work. Just knowing that person will help you identify candidates.

Don't wait until you have a need. Start now with a list of organizations to which you will send your job openings when they become available, and, most important, a list of diverse candidates you can contact when you need to hire.

A friend that is an African American female and CEO of a hospital told me how she was recruited. After she finished a presentation the CEO of a competing company introduced himself and said, "I am going to hire you. I don't have a position yet, but when I do I am going to hire you." She told me that CEO kept a very simple list of great candidates and when a position opened he called the people on his list. You should do the same thing.

5. *Interview Four Candidates*

Whenever possible, interview four candidates, include two diverse candidates, and the odds of you hiring a diverse candidate becomes 50%. It levels the playing field and helps to ameliorate any unconscious bias.

I recommend this process based on a 2016 *Harvard Business Review* article that showed that if there's only one woman in your candidate pool, there's statistically little chance she'll be hired—the same applies to race and ethnicity.

Conclusion: Diversity will make you more innovative and add to your bottom line. Hire fast because you have done the work to include diverse candidates.

—Jason Thompson, VP diversity and inclusion
at Techstars

How Do I Manage All These Salespeople?

At this point you'll want to schedule one-on-one meetings with each salesperson, as well as a weekly pipeline review meeting that includes everyone. Running your pipeline review meeting early on may feel a little squishy as everyone is getting up to speed. Once you settle in it should be focused on, at least, top companies progressing through the pipeline, companies about to become customers, prospects at risk of falling out of the funnel, and any other urgent customer-related matters. I also recommend spending time in the beginning of the meeting reviewing key performance indicators (KPIs) to review how the group is doing and so everyone can see how they are doing relative to everyone else. I'd also save a little time at the end of the meeting to talk about general learnings and areas for improvement. This could be process, systems, pitch, communication, pricing, or really anything that is going to help the company grow. This meeting should be scheduled for an hour, though early on it will likely run longer. As you get into a good cadence and rhythm it'll settle back into a 45-minute long weekly meeting.

One question you are probably asking yourself right now is, "Do I make my first hire the manager of the sales group?" The answer is, "It depends." Candidly having four salespeople reporting to you is a *huge* time consumer, but in the early days, as you are still in learning mode, it has many advantages, and most important is that it keeps you really close to the customer. Regardless, depending on your first hire's experience (i.e. they've built early stage companies before and have been in senior leadership positions), it might be appropriate and okay to let that person lead. This is one for which you'll have to use your insight.

The reason "it depends" and you'll need to feel it out is because not all great salespeople can be managers, even if they want to. Salespeople often view management as the obvious career track. For some it's true and others can have successful and healthy career as salespeople. We're not going to cover hiring a manager in this book, but I will share that your first sales management hire is equally as critical to get right as your first sales hire. If you hire the right person, they can transform your business while taking quite a bit of pressure off you. If you hire the wrong person, they can kill your business even if they are great sellers themselves.

If it turns out that you do have three to four direct reports, then it will become important to bring in a head of sales before you hire anyone else. This is important for, at least, two reasons. The first is that as CEO I don't advise that you have more than four sales reports if you want to run the company well. It's not that as CEO you can't handle this many reports, it's just not the greatest use of your time to be managing individual contributors at this point. Now I'm making an assumption here that you've followed this playbook and are actually on the path to scale. If you aren't, then you shouldn't be hiring this many salespeople yet. But if you are, you'll want to be managing the business instead of being inside the business.

Additionally, it's important (and maybe more so) that your sales leader feels like they are building the team versus inheriting one. This gives them more ownership and accountability as you continue to grow. Whenever you do hire your first sales leader they are going to want to put their own stamp on the sales organization, and they should—it's literally why you are hiring them. And especially when hiring early stage sales leaders, you are going to want them to feel like they built and own the sales organization. This allows them the flexibility to work and build in their style, which if they are good means you'll sell more faster, because they'll have their own playbook on growth.

Is It Time to Scale Yet?

Okay, so you now have three to four salespeople and maybe a head of sales. Your new salespeople are up to speed and starting to close some business. You've iterated on your sales process and likely have identified different attributes of what you will look for in future sales hires, so now what? It's time to start proving your ability to scale.

My next step is to double the sales team in one push (if you have four salespeople, hire four more). Use basically the identical process as before and likewise pay close attention and adjust accordingly in real time over their first 60–90 days. The one main difference in hiring this next group is that their short-term/long-term financial motivation will likely tip more toward short-term because now you have more understanding and predictability in your sales cycle and commission structure (we'll get to that shortly). Assuming a fully successful hiring group (big assumption) you now have enough data to start building more predictable models and figuring out your longer-term hiring plans.

The question you are probably asking yourself is, "How will I know when I'm ready to double my sales force?" You might also be wondering about hiring versus cost. Both are the right things to be thinking about.

In terms of how you will know it's time, cost plays into this. Remember that in Chapter 4 we discussed building a sales model. Since you've been diligently keeping up on it, you should have a good understanding of your cost of sales, how long it takes the average salesperson to ramp up, and at what point a salesperson can fund their own salary. By using the model you will know when you can afford to hire more salespeople. Likewise by using your model you will start to have a better understanding of the predictability around sales. When you bring in your next group of sales hires, this should also make it easier to know when someone is doing well and if they just won't cut it in the long term. If you don't have the actual working capital to hire but you have solid metrics and proven traction, then this is a good time to raise money to fund growth.

The final takeaway here for the entire chapter, but especially this last part on scaling beyond your first few hires, is to collect and use data for decision making. Be really diligent about understanding what and why in your own process gives you data-driven confidence that you are ready to scale and then use that same data to help drive decisions on how to scale. If you can do this right, you'll hire a very happy, highly productive sales team focused on helping you build the biggest business possible.

Paying Salespeople

The topic of how to pay a salesperson is usually pretty bifur-cated. This is because often your top salespeople will be some of the highest paid people in your organization (and often higher paid than the CEO). Some people completely believe that it's the salesperson who is out there taking risks and keeping the company funded while others believe that their job, especially with a great product, is easy and therefore salespeople are overcompensated. As someone who made their living building out sales teams in early stage companies, I fall in the camp that top salespeople should be highly compensated and that their compensation should be *heavily* weighted by performance.

What this typically means is that, while a salesperson will usu-ally (though not always) have a base salary like any employee, if they are good, it's only a small part of their total compensation, with the lion's share of their compensation coming from commis-sion. If you aren't familiar with what commission is, commission is a percentage of any closed sale shared with the salesperson. Com-mission percentages can range from very small, such as 1%, to 50% or more, based on several factors including the type of prod-uct, the size of the sale, and the cost of sales to the company, as well as the base salary of the salesperson.

Once you have a more mature sales organization and sales pro-cess and you're able to project sales targets with good accuracy based on historical data, you'll base your commission and entire compensation structure on the overall percentage that your sales organization costs the company—but we're not there yet. Right now, your goal is to find the best people who can sell your prod-uct to the right customer, and pay them enough so that they want to help you grow the biggest company possible.

As a side note, there are some organizations who don't pay sales commissions and instead pay salespeople a higher overall base. We won't be discussing this model in this book, but if that's interesting to you, check out the book *Drive* by Daniel H. Pink. I did experiment with this model once, and what I found was that it doesn't work well in startups where there are dozens of variables in ICP, product, price, the type of salesperson, and pretty much everything else. In addition, startups are typically cash constrained. You need a well-defined sales process and a salesperson profile, a keen ability to hire, and plenty of cash in the bank in order to have a base-salary only sales team.

Traversing Changes in Compensation

To kick off this section, I'm thankful for my friend AJ Bruno who has shared a story from his days at TrendKite:

> "AJ, are you freaking kidding me?" the first externally hired manager I had brought to TrendKite, was apparently not too impressed with what was showing on the screen.
>
> "So, let me just get this straight, our base salary changes monthly based on team size, the amount of variable compensation we make also changes monthly, and you're telling me that my team goal is based on ARR (annual recurring revenue), but our team is tied to bookings?"
>
> It was September 2016, and I was staring at eight angry sales managers in a room where I had just delivered their new compensation plans.
>
> ARR is a software company's lifeblood. It's the ultimate measuring stick in SaaS (Software-as-a-Service) and is considered the "scorecard" for a startup. TrendKite, the PR analytics software company I cofounded in 2012, had cultivated this lifeblood very well in its first four years of existence and was one of the fastest growing software companies in the United States by the end of 2017. The average IPO company see growth numbers of 30% year-over-year. TrendKite had averaged 250% growth per year over a four year period.
>
> My manager was succinctly bringing to my attention the main problem with their new compensation plans: while managers were switching their "measuring stick," the individual sellers were not. Individual sellers were still measured off of bookings. If a sales rep sold a discounted two-year deal for $20,000, the manager would be credited $10,000 ARR ($20 000/2 years). It was in the manager's best interest to get the rep to sell the deal for one year at

$12,000, but a rep's best interest to not to do that. Long story short, their goals were not aligned.

Lesson number one: always align goals across the company.

I had to brace for what I was about to say next. I hadn't been the driver in creating this plan. I had let others in the organization take the wheel and personally felt like the plan was Frankensteined together, and that was completely on me.

How did we end up here? Our compensation plans at day one were super straightforward. You got 10% on every deal sold, $1,000 for hitting your monthly quota, and $1,000 for hitting your quarterly quota. Simple enough, right? And it absolutely was. In 2016 we had 21 out of 25 individual sellers hit their yearly quota target.

So what happened in the next two years that changed? Our sales and account management teams were now 100-plus people and when you grow you find out quickly that there are a lot of stakeholders that have influence on your decisions (as there should be). How you manage this is critical.

The CEO, VP of finance, head of operations, and HR manager will all be interested in how you are paying your people and how it affects their part of the business. The board and the investors will want to make sure that the rollup of the financials connect to the "unit economics" of the company (in simple terms unit economics is how much you make for every dollar sold in a scaled business). Lastly, you will read a lot about what other thought leaders and market trends are saying. Ultimately, it is on you to collect the data and drive the process.

Lesson number two: lean into building compensation plans, and make sure you are the driver of the overall plan.

Every quarter it became the exercise of "is this the behavior that we should be optimizing for?" Being a founder who had taken on the role of the company's chief sales leader had always been fun. I didn't feel the pressure of a traditional "VP of sales" because I knew I could always find a role within the organization. I felt empowered to bridge the gap between the science of sales (board level, scaled up) and the art of it (individual sellers and the month-to-month, quarter-to-quarter psychology behind it). But at this very moment, I felt helpless and not in control of the major output for the team—their sales compensation. Because of this, how in the world could I feel in control of the results?

And the answer was that I didn't. Taking a step back for a second and looking at how we got to that point, it was pretty simple.

There's a great article by Dave Kellogg that discusses the merits of how much "cushion" a company should have between total quota and the financial plan that is approved at the board level. If you have $100,000 quota, and your financial target is $80,000, that's a 20% cushion.

Dave had this to say: "So think about this for a minute. The VP of sales can be at 83% of quota, the sales managers on average can be at 71% of quota, and the sales reps can be at 63% of their quota—and the CEO will still be on plan. The only people hitting their number, making their on-target earnings (OTE), and drinking champagne at the end of the quarter are the CEO and CFO. (And they better drink it in a closet.)

That's why I believe cushion isn't just a math problem. It's a cultural issue. Do you want a "Let them eat cake" or a "We're all in this together" culture? The answer to that question should help determine how much cushion you have and where it lives." (See https://kellblog.com/2018/01/23/quota-over-assignment-and-culture/.)

TrendKite had the opposite issue for the first two years scaling its new business revenue: our quotas were below financial plan! Why? Because of the successful growth, there was downward pressure to hire fast, but I held back to find the right people. So, our quota capacity (the aggregate of the individual quotas) was typically 20% under the plan during that time. But guess what? We hit plan almost every single month (34/36 months). So think about that, our sellers were producing 120% of what they were supposed to, so that everyone won.

We had one of the best sales team in all of Austin and I would have put my team next to any in the country at that time. Everyone was aligned.

Lesson number three: create a system where everyone can win.

Back to my meeting, where cooler heads were prevailing. My second sales hire, who would go on to become the first director of sales at TrendKite, was walking everyone back from the edge of a cliff. "If you guys look at the upside, we now have an accelerator and we are responsible for only 90% of our team's quota to hit our on-target earnings."

This was true, there was more upside. The company's third sales hire, who eventually was promoted to sales manager and also became the director of sales development, also spoke up "Plus, all of the OTEs have gone up."

I could count on these two to help the rest of the team understand the changes and how to maximize their compensation as the plan evolved; however, other salespeople weren't as convinced. They looked over at my most senior leader, someone I had worked with for the past six years spanning two companies and two cities, for validation. She was deep in thought. She was the most pragmatic of the bunch but the least diplomatic. The other managers looked over as well. I held my breath as she mulled it over. She let out a sigh and said "AJ., even though there are quite a few changes, I can get onboard with them."

In that moment, I had crossed the chasm…

—AJ Bruno, founder and former sales leader at TrendKite and founder of Quotepath

Let's start with a few facts.

Fact 1: Whatever Compensation Structure You Set Up, It Will Change

Sometimes annually and sometimes more often, whatever compensation structure has been set up is going to change. The reason is that the more you learn more about your business and what it takes to drive the business, you will need to make adjustments so that both the business and the salesperson can make money. It would be great to simply set a flat commission rate on day one and leave it forever, but what you will learn is that it may be too high, too low, or the wrong structure all together. For example, early on in many SaaS companies salespeople will be paid a flat commission in perpetuity for any sales that they close. That's a great motivator for early salespeople because they are building a valuable book of business. While that salesperson will be well compensated over time, the challenge with that model is that one of two things will typically happen. First, at some point the salesperson is making so much money they don't really have any motivation to sell new customers. In this case, they are being highly compensated yet not doing their core job of bringing new business into the company. The other byproduct of this model is the converse, which is that they are still doing a great job bringing new business into the company but neglecting their old customers and still getting paid. While this type of commission structure is fairly common early on (and actually what I would recommend), over time those companies will need to change the compensation structure so that legacy customers don't pay as high (or any) commissions and salespeople stay motivated to bring in new customers while legacy ones can be managed by a different group. It's fine for commission plans to change regularly, and anyone who's been in sales for any amount of time will expect it as long as you set the tone up from day one. Make it clear both verbally and in writing that their plan is subject to change and that your goal is to maximize dollars for both the business and them.

Fact 2: Salespeople Like to Make Money

If they don't, you probably didn't hire that person into the right job. This may seem obvious, however, I'm stating this because no matter how much your top salespeople make, they will always want to make more. Just be prepared for it. They will be looking for ways to game the system; they'll argue with you to make more commissions and fight for deals. While the day to day of this may not seem attractive, this, in most cases, is the behavior you want because it also means that they will work hard to close the highest value sales possible. And knowing that they will try to "game" the system to make more money is a great thing, because as you create new commission plans, you can create structures where gaming the system is win/win for you and them.

Let me give you an example: when I created the commission plan at Business.com, there were two behaviors we wanted to encourage. The first was volume of new customers and the second was customers that did not churn in the first five months. At the stage of our business at that time, we had been growing revenue steadily for about a year, but our customer count was flat because our churn was pretty high, around 15% monthly. We also had enough historical data to show that if a customer stayed at least four months, they were likely to stay for greater than 15 months. I created a simple matrixed plan that paid out a set commission for all sales based on the number of new customers each month. At certain new customer thresholds that commission number would go up for all new customers. What this did was incentivize our salespeople on volume because there was a multiplying effect of breaking through to the next new customer threshold.

We saw an immediate jump in new customers and almost doubled our customer count to several thousand within a year. The second part of the matrix was how we paid commissions. The commission percentage went up as our salespeople sold to more customers, and it also went up for every month a customer stayed a customer. What this did was incentivize our salespeople to focus on quality in the increased volume of new customers. This resulted in our churn improving from around 15% to less than 3% within that same year, which also had a multiplying effect on our total customer count.

Fact 3: Generally Speaking, Salespeople Are Needy, Have Big Egos, and Have Some Insecurity

I say this as a salesperson who has personally exhibited needy, insecure qualities at some point in my sales career. Now I'm guessing that there are some salespeople reading this right now, maybe even friends of mine, who think "not me"—well, sorry, but I do mean you, too. And it's okay, it's normal. Why am I bringing this up in a section about compensation? Because your compensation conversations is where these attributes will come out the most. Compensation conversations are difficult to hold with any employee and no matter how long you've been having them, but salespeople are a different kind of animal here. Keep in mind, they negotiate money and trade value all day long, and it's in their blood.

Figuring Out a Fair Base and Commission

On to compensation: if you've ever asked anyone how to compensate salespeople and they have a seemingly standard answer, ignore it. The truth is, like figuring out product–market fit, it's a process. It will depend on the sales process, price, margins, the product, the market, your location, the type of person you are hiring, cost of sales and service, and LTV (lifetime value of your customers). The place to start is, what is a fair base that allows the salesperson to comfortably pay their bills and not struggle (assuming a reasonable lifestyle) in your region. While you definitely want your salespeople to be hungry and motivated, you don't want them to suffer month to month as that will lead to them leaving—especially your best ones. You want them to make enough money in their base so that they are comfortable enough, but with a big carrot (commission) out there so they can potentially make enough money to stay motivated.

Next you will want to think about the overall compensation package when commission is considered. Check out similar product/sale types as general starting points, but again assume that this will be adjusted. See what top salespeople for similar types of products are making. You'll also want to consider the stage of your business, what behaviors you are trying to motivate, and most important the cash your business has and what you will need to stay in business and keep growing.

There are many different types of sales plans, and as I keep saying, it'll take time to figure out which is the best one for your company—and it will change. Do your best to start simple and as I also keep saying, set the expectation with your salespeople that the commission plan will change as the business matures.

		5	10	15
MRR Bookings	>$25k	10%	12%	15%
	$20k–$25k	10%	12%	12%
	$15k–$20k	7%	10%	10%
	<$15k	7%	7%	10%

New Customers

Figure 5.3   Commission Payout Matrix
Source: Courtesy of Austin Dressen.

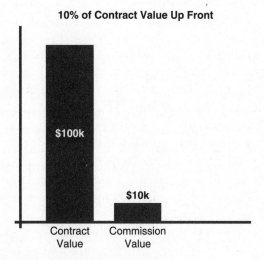

10% of Contract Value Up Front

$100k

$10k

Contract
Value

Commission
Value

Figure 5.4   Commission Payout—Up Front
Source: Courtesy of Austin Dressen.

Figures 5.3, 5.4, and 5.5 show three examples of sales plans. Keep in mind as you look at them, they are meant to be general frameworks not specific recommendations. The percentages and time frames will vary based on the specifics of your business.

I'm personally a big believer that my top salespeople should be the highest compensated around (relative to peer salespeople/products) *when* they are performing. Conversely, when they

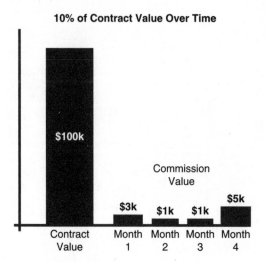

Figure 5.5 Commission Payout—Success-Based
Source: Courtesy of Austin Dressen.

are not performing, they should feel it in their compensation, too. What this means is that, I want to pay them a base that's enough for them to live on *and* have the ability to make more money than their peers through commissions. This creates a culture of highly motivated, low-churn top performers that also makes it easy to weed out low performers—often self-selecting their exits because they aren't making good money compared to their peers.

The challenge with my theory, at least for the first few hires, is you just don't have enough sales data yet to know how much commission someone will make. You don't really know yet how long the sales cycle is, and you don't know how many new customers a salesperson can close in a month. You are still playing with price and your product is still new enough that you won't have a good grasp on churn. The best you can really do is to take an educated guess, be honest about it, and don't be afraid to make adjustments to the commission plan (in either direction) as you learn more.

For your first few sales hires, this is also why hiring people with a more long-term financial mindset is important. Your first few salespeople will likely be positively lopsided with equity relative to every other salesperson who joins you (even numbers four through eight). Those first three to four salespeople are taking the biggest compensation risk, and for that risk they should have bigger upside potential. It also helps them be more bought in and help to drive a culture of positive growth. The bigger potential plays out in two ways. The first is direct with earlier access to the best potential customers. This is probably pretty obvious, but if you are selling to the Fortune 500 companies and you are one of the first few salespeople, you are likely identifying and working with the highest potential ones.

The other way early salespeople are compensated is with larger equity grants. Assuming that you are a company who uses equity to help compensate and motivate your employees, then salespeople will receive equity as well. Salespeople hired later are usually given smaller amounts of equity compensation relative to other departments because they have the ability to make more money through commission, but those early sales hires are taking a bigger risk and will likely be given a larger equity grant.

You probably get the pattern here, but just like identifying your ICP, figuring out pricing, building your first sales model, your first few passes on your commission plan are not likely to be right. The more important factor is developing something that feels fair and equitable around targets that the salespeople believe are achievable, and then being transparent that as the company grows and we learn more we will continue to make adjustments to continually align business growth with salesperson compensation.

Chapter 6

Big Businesses Are Built after the Sale Is Closed

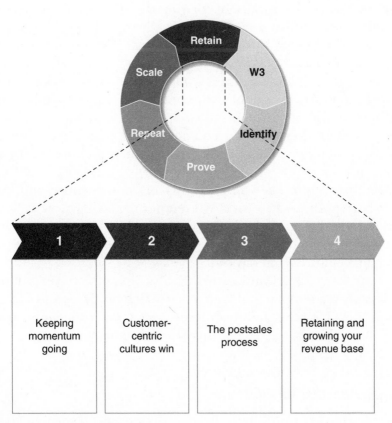

Figure 6.1 Retaining Your Customers

Keeping the Momentum Going

I love writing about this topic. I love it because I attribute a lot of my early success to realizing and identifying how important it is to develop an ongoing relationship with your customers, and more specifically creating some sort of client service department inside your company. It's my experience that a lot of the best salespeople and many founders miss this up front and it isn't until they realize that there is a churn issue that they do something about it—and often that's too late.

Developing an ongoing relationship with your customers is imperative and it's important for you, the reader, to understand that the growth of your company actually starts here! Even if you have the greatest salespeople in the world, if you don't care for your customers, listen to your customers, and appreciate your customers, they will know and they will leave when someone better comes along. If you do take the time to be a good vendor and partner, then your customers will help you grow in many ways, like being patient when things aren't going well, telling their friends and peers at other companies about you and most important staying a customer.

In this chapter we will cover (1) customer-centric cultures, (2) what a postsales process is, (3) retention, and (4) growing your revenue base (Figure 6.1). The goal for you is to start thinking about this early on and make this part of both your sales and company culture from day one.

I'm going to start with a story that touches directly on all four. This is my version of it and I am positive that my peers and superiors at this time have slightly different views or recollections of all this (it was 17 years ago), but this is how I remember it.

Paying Attention after the Sale

I had started with HotJobs in June of 1999 as one of the first 20 or so salespeople in the San Francisco office. At that time HotJobs was one of the pioneers in online recruiting. Today it's fairly standard for people to look for a job online at Indeed, Zip Recruiter or any other number of job websites but back in 1999 there were only a few companies doing that and HotJobs was one of the biggest.

We had our initial public offering that summer and by fall of 1999 I was asked, along with a peer, to join one of the managers in opening the Los Angeles office. We arrived in LA on January 2, 2000, prior to the infamous internet bubble popping of 2000, in which tons and tons of VC-backed, high-valuation companies all came crashing down and were going out of business. My two peers and I were crushing on the sales side. We were all closing record amounts of new customers each month, making boatloads of money in commissions, and (almost) everyone we hired came on and kicked ass as well. We were all very happy, going out for expensive dinners, driving nice cars and not really thinking about the happiness of our new customers.

After about 8 months of this (and 14 months of being a sales-person for HotJobs) I was starting to get bored with the same job day in and day out. As I started to slow down, I picked up my head and realized that many of our customers were not renewing their contracts when their term was up. We weren't really feeling it in our commission because we were replacing churned customers with new customers at a faster rate, but it was clearly a problem for HotJobs in the long term.

There were actually two problems, but only one that I solved. The first problem was the comp plan (this is not the one I solved at HotJobs, although I did learn a lot that I carried with me to Business.com and beyond), which was to say that the sales team compensation didn't encourage long-term customers. The way we were paid was for new sales in perpetuity with little regard for what happened after a prospect became a customer. Remember in Chapter 5 when I talked about early commission plans? This was the first example, which works well in the early days but as the company goals change to maintaining low churn and happy customers, this commission model no longer works and needs to be fixed.

The second problem, which is what I identified and eventually solved, was that the cause of customer churn was our lack of any real customer service. We did have a small, reactive, call center to work with unhappy customers; however, there was no person responsible for working with our customers once they signed a contract. That means that we did not have a process or dedicated person to onboard them. We didn't have any process for ongoing training and communication, and of course we had no structure to deal with unhappy customers. We had no indication of when a customer was unhappy, and when we had customer churn, we had no idea why. In fact, we lost many customers who were happy because one of our competitors promised them "dedicated help" in the form of personal attention.

Our product was great and even though I was clearly biased, I did think it was the best in class. However, it was a very competitive time for job search companies, with Monster, Careerbuilder, and many others on a land grab for new customers. Through all this we had literally *no* postsales process or even a team who focused on it. In the fall of 2000 I raised my hand and asked if I could create a team in Los Angeles focused not only on customer service but on owning renewals and up-sells. The CEO and VP of sales were open to the experiment and let me go.

I started by putting a basic postsales process in place in Los Angeles which was a series of simple touch points with new customers from day one through the first year. In the first few weeks those touch points were focused on onboarding, training, and making sure that the new customers were using our platform, finding success, and not getting hung up. As the customer matured, those touch points became a combination of check-ins to make sure we were meeting their goals, ongoing education, and new product training to keep them engaged and happy. I hired/trained a small team in Los Angeles and within just a few months we saw incredible results as our churn dramatically dropped and our up-sells dramatically grew. I can't remember all the specifics, but my boss and the CEO were pleased enough with the results that they immediately promoted me and turned me loose on the rest of the sales organization.

By this time we had opened up offices in several more cities including Austin, Boston, Washington, DC, Chicago, Miami, and of course we still had offices in San Francisco and New York. Many of the offices did have some sort of inbound customer service team, which I inherited and retrained. After roughly another quarter, the company's churn issue all but disappeared and the LTV (lifetime value) of our customer was increasing dramatically. It was obvious to my boss and the senior leadership team that the work we were doing was paying off, and I was given a big raise, new title, awards at our president's club, and was told that the company hit profitability several quarters earlier than planned because of this shift.

* * *

I felt this was a relevant story and a good way to introduce this chapter because I see time and time again that companies can get very good at selling and pay virtually no attention to what happens after the sale. And in many cases this can be the death of a company. Over the course of this chapter we spend a lot of time thinking and developing ways to deliver world-class customer service so that you can continue to grow compounding revenue and build a big company.

In the next few sections I talk about customer-centric cultures, the postsales process, retention, and growing your revenue base. I'm going to use a few titles interchangeably. I refer to employees who work with customers after a salesperson hands them off as customer service, client services, and account management. All of these employees have one thing in common, they typically work with paying customers, whereas a salesperson works with prospects as they become customers (and for some time after). In reality there are some important subtle and not-so-subtle differences between those titles and in some cases your business might have two or three of them. For the purposes of this book I'm using them as a marker for any person who works with your customers *after* a sales has been made and *after* the original salesperson is no longer the main point of contact.

Customer-Centric Cultures Win

How can you build an organization that is customer-centric and has high retention with growing lifetime value (LTV)? It starts with culture and it starts from day one.

First, you must understand that without customers you have no business and that your number one job is to provide value to your customers beyond what anyone else can. I know on the surface that sounds obvious but it needs to be something you believe way down in your core. Think back to the day you decided to start your business. It doesn't matter what your original motivation was for starting a business, you believed that you were solving a problem for a particular customer and that you could do that better than anyone. As you start to build your business, developing tech, hiring, fundraising, and all of the other things you need to do to get your business off the ground, it often is forgotten that really you are here to make your customer's life easier and allow them to make more money. Don't let that slip away—it needs to be your guiding light.

If you do truly believe this on day one and continue to remind yourself, it will permeate through your decision making and trickle down to all of your employees. It'll be a part of your root culture, which in turn will help ensure you are building products and a company which not only will delight your customers but will help them win—and help you win.

Your customers are the reason you exist, and this fact should be woven deep into your company culture. This doesn't mean "the customer is always right"—what it means is that your mission should be to deliver the highest quality product and service so that your customer screams from the mountaintops how awesome you and your company are! It starts with the CEO and trickles down. It needs be part of your company values. It even needs to be evident in your commission plans structure. Remember in Chapter 5 when I described the Business.com compensation structure? There were two main drivers for salespeople to make money. The first was bringing new customers onto the platform. The second was making sure they stayed over a specific time threshold, because we knew it meant we had a happy customer. Our sales team knew that long before their account was handed off to the postsales team, that customer had to be happy and set up for long-term success. That set up our account managers to start working with customers who were already happy and seeing success, which made the account managers happy and their job easier and in turn made it even easier to please our customers.

Simply put, having a customer-centric culture must be core to your business if you want to build a big, long-term, and sustainable business. When you do this well, sales becomes easier, revenue grows faster, investors write (bigger) checks and everyone makes more money. When you do this poorly, you fight an uphill battle with customer growth, people question the value of your product (even if it's great), and everyone makes less money.

The Postsales Process

In addition to building a culture from day one that is customer-centric, having a really solid postsale process sets the foundation for delighting your customer. There are a couple of reasons for this. First, this is your blueprint for how your team will work with your customers indefinitely. It might be hard to envision this before you have your first customer or in your first year of having customers, but as your business matures you should have a regular plan and cadence for how you will interact with your customers. When you have this plan it becomes much easier to hire, train, and project revenue for your existing book of business, which is critical in projecting the company's health. Likewise if you plan to raise venture money, having this plan in place will give you data and confidence that is critical to giving your future investors and board confidence in your company's health.

To explore that for a minute, start with hiring your customer service team. We can return to Chapter 1 and the discussion of W3. If you know *who* your customer is, *what* they are buying, and *why* they buy it, *and* you have a clear plan on how to work with them, it becomes very clear who you should be hiring to work with your existing and growing book of business. You'll learn the level of experience your postsales employees will need as well as their general characteristics, similar to how you thought about hiring for salespeople.

It also makes training a new postsales team easier because your postsales process is their job. Of course there will be nuances from customer to customer and they still need to learn about your product, but 80% of their job will be to go through a well-defined process with each one of your customers, based on where they are in their lifecycle. And as your business grows large, you'll even be able to start collecting data on the types of issues, challenges, and opportunities you will have with each individual customer based on the life of their business and how you impact their growth. And while this may seem far off now and certainly not on your current product roadmap, starting early by focusing on a postsales process will enable you and your team to help your customers be more successful, which means you win too.

This leads me to my last point, which is being able to project the revenue and health of your business. Stop and think about that pragmatically for a minute. In Chapter 4 we talk about early sales modeling as a means to understand and measure how your salespeople perform and your assumptions around customer growth. New customer growth is only half the equation—and in the long term, it is much less than half.

During the first year or maybe longer you will be heavily focused on acquiring new customers, and in many cases you'll have more new customer revenue than existing, but it sneaks up quickly. Once you start to find repeatability in your sales process, and especially once you start hiring more than one or two salespeople, suddenly your existing customer base (or "book of business") quickly outweighs the new revenue that your salespeople are bringing in monthly. And just as in your sales process, which you need to be able to predict new revenue, you need to understand how your existing customers will perform so that you can project how your entire business is doing and will do in the future. Having a postsales process gives you the data to understand how your customers behave, so that you can project the future and plan for growth.

It's not only important for your company that your team has a clear blueprint, it's also important for your customers. In many ways, the relationship you are developing with your customers is no different from any relationship. When you first get to know someone, you want to like them and trust that everyone has the best intentions. As time goes on, if you don't stay in contact with that person, any familiarity fades away. The difference here is that with your customers you can (and should) take advantage of your business relationship, which allows you to set clear expectations.

I've managed both the sales and postsales teams at HotJobs, Business.com, BlackLocus, and Joust, and one thing that I did at all four which proved to be very successful for customer satisfaction was having a dedicated section of the training and onboarding part of the postsales process focused on what kind of communication each customer should expect and at what cadence for the life of their contract (and beyond). We did this both verbally and in writing so that if the customer ever had a question about "what's next," they had an easy reference. Aside from great transparency into the process, a byproduct of sharing the communication cadence is that it cuts down on nonemergency service calls, because our customers knew there was a planned touchpoint at which they could talk about anything outside the ordinary.

Building a Postsales Process

In many ways, the fundamentals of building your postsales process are no different from building your sales process. As your company matures you need to go through all the same steps in identifying common items, issues, and opportunities for customer touch points. The one advantage to building our postsales process is that it's hard to guess wrong at your first one as long as you are being diligent. Over time every business will vary based on its unique characteristics, but in the beginning the act of simply putting a basic postsales process in place will give your team and your customers the highest probability for success.

To get you started, I'm sharing with you the process I implemented at Business.com. By the time I took over this department we had hundreds of customers and over $10 million in sales, which meant we had plenty of data to build this process fairly accurately from the start. Even so, starting with a structure something like this and then adapting as you learn more about your customers is a good place to start. We had six basic steps that allowed us to work with a customer indefinitely:

Step 1: Welcome Email within Two Hours after Sale Is Closed

I can't stress enough how important this first contact is. Someone just put themselves out there with their boss and agreed to give you money. Thank them and welcome them to your family. Make them feel, right away, that they are valued!

Keep this email short. Welcome them, thank them for their business, provide any immediate or urgent information, and tell them about next steps, which for us included someone reaching out to schedule onboarding training. It's okay for this email to be automated, but it shouldn't feel that way.

Step 2: Schedule Onboarding and Training

Depending on your product and company, onboarding and training could be as little as anything from a login and a few video links to a multiday onsite training. At Business.com we could typically onboard and train a client in an hour phone call. We made sure to reach out to every new customer, personally, within 12 hours to schedule this call. You want to do this quickly because your product is still new and exciting to your new customer and you want them to start using it right away. No matter how excited they are, building new habits is hard for anyone, and the more you can help your customer to build new, positive habits around your product, the higher the likelihood they will have success early on. Try to schedule this meeting as soon as possible after the sale closes, so that your new customer's excitement and enthusiasm around your product is still fresh. This will help with keeping them engaged and getting the most out of that meeting.

Step 3: Twenty-Four Hour Check-in after Your Training Meeting

This check-in, to me, is as important as your welcome email. You just took an hour or more of someone's time to get them onboarded, but for them it's all new. They probably retained the basics but also it's probable that many of the details, even important ones, about how to use your product are easily forgotten. This should be a nonintrusive and short email. Early on, before you have many customers, it will likely be more general and say something like, "I wanted to check in to see if you have any questions or are running into any roadblocks." As your business matures and you add more customers and data, you can start to be more specific with follow-ups around areas that commonly need more help. This check-in continues to set the tone that you are a customer-centric organization and are here to help make sure your customer is successful.

Step 4: Day 7 and Day 14 Check-ins

These check-ins should be a little more in-depth than your 24-hour check-in. By this time, your new customer should be using your product and you should be able to see what they are doing and get a sense of how often they are using it, relative to your expectations. At Business.com these two check-ins were less scripted; over time we used actual data on how our customer was using the product to drive what we were checking in about.

Step 5: Month 1, 2, and 3 Account Reviews

At Business.com account reviews were much different than check-ins. They were more proactive and in the best cases more strategic. We essentially developed a process over time of preparing reports based on our customers goals to see how they did looking back and came up with a plan for improvement (even when goals were being met) going forward. In Chapter 5 I talk about our five-month threshold, we knew that if customers stayed at least five months that they would be with us for over 24 months. Because of this we explicitly built into our postsales process a monthly account review up until that point. This not only enabled us to help our customers continually improve over those first months but also developed relationships with our customers that showed we cared about the success of their business.

Step 6: Move to Quarterly Account Reviews and 45-Day Check-ins.

Once we crossed the third monthly account review, we would move to quarterly in-depth account reviews. We did this because our data suggested that after three months, most of our clients had a good understanding of how we work together and there was less movement and volatility in their accounts. Those quarterly reviews, like the monthly ones, were typically scheduled for an hour. Between those quarterly meetings, we would still generate spot reports and send them a check-in email every 45 days. This allowed us to have ongoing communication with our customers that was light but still kept us top of mind and also provided value on an ongoing basis.

This is just one example and your experience may vary greatly; the point is that a process is important (and expect your process to change as you collect data and learn more). As part of your process, there should always be an opportunity to collect feedback. All of this—the process, notes on each step, the feedback—should be housed in your CRM, the same one that your salespeople are using, and ideally in a way that you can pull data and evolve the process over time.

Retention and Growing Your Revenue Base

If there is one mistake that I most consistently see SaaS businesses making, it is not investing in the customer success function early enough. It is so natural to view ARR growth as the singular most important thing for your startup at the early stage (we all love growth!), but that is far from the truth and churn kills more business than a lack of growth.

Where most founders get into trouble is not understanding the complexity and volume of challenges that they will face as their customer base scales. Why does this happen so frequently? Early on, there are a small number of customers that you spent a greater than average amount of time selling and qualifying before getting on board. The growth continues and the customer base along with their needs becomes more diverse in nature. At the same time, on the other side of the house, your sales and marketing teams are becoming less careful in qualifying new customers because they now have these new lofty sales goals. All of the sudden churn picks up and you're being reactive with customer success hires and changes to your support and success processed. You now have a leaky bucket problem.

One thing that I try to impress upon founders early on is to reframe the churn number as a CAC [customer acquisition cost] number. Everyone understands CAC, and how expensive and challenging it is to get a new customer on, but churn mistakenly isn't viewed with as much importance or urgency. Let's use an example. Assume your startup as $1M of ARR and you just churned $100K last quarter (10% quarterly, 40% annualized). Let's also assume that your average contract value is $20K and *your CAC is $12K. So, a $100K churn quarter is the equivalent of five customers ($100K/$20K). Therefore, your CAC just to maintain your current ARR in that quarter was $60K. Put differently, your sales team spent their time closing five new customers just to break even in that period. In many markets $60K is nearly the entire annual salary for one customer success rep that could have been working to prevent this churn, and also make many of your other customers even happier in the period.*

—Michael Gilroy, partner at Canaan Ventures

Throughout the entire book I've referenced churn and customer retention as key factors in growing your business. And throughout this entire chapter l've described how building a customer-centric company enables you to grow your revenue base faster. Now we'll bring it all together.

When you build a customer-centric organization and you have a clearly defined postsales process, something magical happens—your customer retention becomes very strong, which in turn strengthens your revenue base and your LTV. The *why* is probably pretty obvious: you have happy customers who value your product and your company and they feel valued by you. But how will you know if your retention is good or great or bad? How can you tell if your revenue base is growing or shrinking?

Keep Being Metrics Driven

A common issue I see in companies of all stages is that while they know their top-line retention metrics, such as, "We lose X% of our customers per month," that's where it ends. Too many founders and sales leaders don't pay close enough attention to downstream metrics early on. For example, which features of your product do your customers use, and how do individual customers differ from the norm on feature usage? Ask the same question for over-all product engagement: how often do all your customers login or engage with your product, and how do your individual customers each engage, relative to the norm? Can you find commonalities around engagement and LTV? And what system do you have in place to measure customer sentiment?

Similar to how you are building out a metrics-driven business and metrics-driven sales organization, your client service organization also needs to be highly metrics focused. At maturity, you should be able to predict, by customer type, maximum spend, and time frame in which revenue will grow, potential churn points by customer type and product type, and any other data that helps drive your business. Not only do *you* need to know it, this should be a center point for your postsales team to focus on and these metrics should be known companywide.

Just like the weekly pipeline meeting you have with your salespeople, you will want to also set up a weekly book-of-business review. This meeting should be both quantitative and qualitative, meaning that from day one you should have a strong opinion about the metrics that matter most to predicting customer happiness and potential growth (the quantitative part), as well as anecdotal data on why customers are happy and why they use certain features or don't, as well as what enhancements they'd like to see. Each employee should know and be responsible for (along with their manager) their own actual book-of-business value, potential value of their book of business, time needed to maximize each account within their book of business, and all the potential hurdles specific to your business of achieving maximum book value.

This metrics-driven mindset starts on day one of your company, day one of your first customer sold, day one of your first client service hire, and should be prevalent inside of the entire organization.

Postsales Is Critical to Retention

The second part of developing strong customer retention and growing your revenue base is leveraging your postsales team as another sales channel. Some people might argue against this concept and even say it's contradictory to being customer-centric, however, I believe strongly that every person in your company who interfaces with a customer should have some responsibility around revenue growth. In my experience, the key to balancing revenue growth with happy customers is every piece in this book leading up to now:

A. Have the right customers for your product— the *who* in W3.
B. Your customers are buying the right product— the *what* in W3.
C. Measure the value being traded—the *why* in W3.
D. Develop the right process to identify, sell, and close those customers—Chapters 2, 3, 4.
E. Have a customer-centric culture—knowing when, how, and why to engage with your customers.
F. Understand how to measure both happiness and potential, through collected data and regular reviews.

Then when it comes time for your postsales team member to talk to your customers about renewals, up-sells, and new products, your customers will trust you, and "selling" them won't actually be "selling," but working together to optimize your customer's own potential.

Let's go back to the story in Chapter 2 about my time at BlackLocus. Once we had identified our W3 at BlackLocus (A, B, and C), we quickly realized two things. The first was that our price points were going to be much higher than originally thought. When I joined, BlackLocus was charging between $100 and $1,000 per month based on customer size. Once we figured out our W3, our contract value went up and was $10,000 per month on the low end and $150,000 per month on the high end. With contract values that high, most customers wanted to test their way to full-scale, and understandably so, considering we were still a pretty young company.

Since we knew we were usually not optimizing account size on day one (which was typically mutually acknowledged and eventually became part of our sales and onboarding plan), it was imperative that we had a clear way for our customers and us to measure the value being traded as well as a clear process on how to work together to identify what worked, what didn't, and where there was opportunity for our customers to maximize the value they received from us (C, D, E, and F).

By working with our customers in this way, we knew on day one that if we didn't provide visibility into how our customer was doing and where they could make improvements to their business, we would never maximize that customer's potential—and we couldn't do that without working with our customers since ultimately they were the ones who knew how their business was being impacted. We set up regular account review and optimization meetings with every customer and, in the case of BlackLocus, biweekly and monthly for the first six months. This resulted in maximizing account opportunity with the majority of our customers within the first four months. And because we worked so closely with our customers we knew both what that maximum value would be and how we were impacting their business on a regular basis—because they'd tell us (again, C–F).

In the early days of your company, before you have any customers, all of your revenue comes from every new customer you bring into your organization. As time goes on, however, more and more of your revenue and revenue growth will come from your existing customer base. As a fully mature company it's not uncommon for 80% or more of your revenue to come from existing customers. Knowing this upfront, creating a culture that focuses on customer satisfaction, and putting systems in place early on to foster and maximize those relationships will set you up for building a long-term and highly valuable business!

Chapter 7

Now Go Out and Sell More Faster!

Okay, we made it! Congratulations and, more important, thank you for taking the time to read *Sell More Faster.*

When I first started pulling together the concepts for this book in the summer of 2018, my intention wasn't to actually write a book, but to develop a series of simple workshops to help both my portfolio and my peers at Techstars to create some order in the process of identifying product–market fit. I'd regularly get the same two questions, can I "help X company with sales" or "deliver a sales workshop."

I was never really sure what a single workshop on sales would look like. Instead I mapped out what I believed to be the core pieces, to deliver a series of workshops. That work resulted in 18 topics, which are represented in the six chapters you just read. The pieces were all there and what I realized was that I just needed to organize them in a consumable way—eight months later, I'm writing the final chapter of the book.

Looking back to all I wrote, there is one theme that is resonating with me now more than ever and if you, the reader, take only one concept away with you, it's that until you really know your W3 you can't build a big and sustainable business. Sure you might get some early customers because you believe so deeply in your product and the problem you aim to solve, but until you really know *who* your core customer is, *what* they are buying from you (not what you are selling), and *why* they buy it, it's impossible to build a big and scalable business.

The work it takes to truly identify your W3 is hard, tedious, and may take some time—time you think you don't have. However I see it literally every day, when founders are so anxious to show traction as product built or pipeline movement that they don't step back and take the time to make sure they actually know their *who, what,* and *why.* Instead they rush forward more concerned with optics or trying to meet goals "others" think are right or even simply because of the feeling that they are wasting time if they aren't selling or building.

Take the Long View

This is a marathon, and if you are successful you'll be working on your business for a long time. When we invest at the accelerator level, our assumption is that we're in this with you for 10-plus years. There are no shortcuts. It doesn't matter that your friend's company is growing faster than yours or that some company was an "overnight success." Most overnight successes still take close to 10 years. Stop! Race your own race! Take the time to do the hard work on identifying your W3 and be certain about it. If you aren't certain then keep testing until you are—and if you are wrong, start over, because until you nail this the rest of the book is useless.

That's not to say you can't use all the frameworks and lessons in this book to build a sales organization and even look like you have a world-class organization, but if your underlying W3 foundation isn't in place, then you will never be a big business, you'll suffer churn of customers and employees and find yourself spinning on the same issues around growth over and over while someone else comes in and eats your lunch.

Implementing What You've Learned

So what do you do from here? My hope is that while the work is hard, the concepts are simple enough that you can use *Sell More Faster* as a go-to playbook for the entire history of your company. And as you move from stage to stage, you can refer back to each chapter to both confirm that you are on the right path and have a framework for what's next.

Start by taking the time to have a theory of your W3. If you already have that covered, awesome! Now go test it. Remember that in those early days, before you have nailed product–market fit, you are seeking product–market direction through the customer development process and that true "sales" doesn't start until you've found repeatability within your W3. Ask prospective customers lots of question, be curious, be okay with being wrong, a lot, and learn. Your prospects may tell you directly or you may have to infer how to solve their biggest challenges, but take the time to listen. Let your customers lead you on the path to product–market fit. We cover this in Chapter 2.

Once you do start to see signs of product–market direction, take a mental pause and start your early instrumentation. Use your early sales process and sales funnel to prove and disprove why you think your W3 is right. Build an early model around it and track your metrics on a daily and weekly basis. Have an opinion about what growth looks like and use these simple tools to gauge where you are right and wrong. Don't be afraid to adjust as you learn all the places you are wrong, and you will be wrong a lot. And don't be afraid to pivot, based on the information you are now collecting. Chapter 3 covers this.

As the data you are collecting starts to solidify and you start to feel some product–market direction, use the techniques and concepts in Chapter 4 so that you can start bringing in early revenue. Learn about what is important to your buyer(s), how they value your product, and start to look for early signs of repeatability—all the while refining your sales process and model. And remind yourself (over and over) that building a big company is not about "set it and forget it" but a constant iteration and often a reinvention of what you are doing and how you are doing it.

And then, when you are starting to see repeatability in your sales process, and, more important, can clearly communicate that repeatability, what works, and what you still need to learn, bring in your first outside salesperson to prove yourself right or wrong. Work together to continually refine the process and likely even your W3. And when you've started to see, with data, that repeatability conveyed to that first hire, refer back to Chapter 5 and follow the disciplined approach to growing your sales team on the path to repeatability, product–market fit, and growing a huge and successful business.

And finally, remember your job isn't over when the sale is closed; it's really just starting. As you start to have a real customer base remember that while your business grows from new customers, your business is built upon your growing customer base. Read and reread Chapter 6 and embody a customer-centric culture from day one. Always remember that if you continue to focus on building value for and delighting your customers, they will stay with you, continue to buy from you, and tell their friends how awesome your company is.

Revel in Your Passion

I've lived this journey both as an operator and now as managing director for Techstars Austin, working with new startups every year. I know firsthand how hard this is. Personally I revel in it. I love it! And you should too. If you are truly passionate about building your business and solving your customer's problems, you have to love the process. The principles and frameworks in this book are not the only way to build a big, long-term, and successful business, but they are the ones that have worked for me and the concepts we share with our portfolio. And just like all the concepts in this book, this entire book is and will always be in constant iteration. So as you go out and test and grow your business, pay it back to me and forward to others by sharing how you are refining your process.

So that's it. I hope you've enjoyed and, more important, found real value in this book. Now it's your turn to get out there and *sell more faster.*

About the Author

Amos was born in the Bronx, New York, and grew up in Fort Lee, New Jersey. At a young age, Amos started seeking adventure and pushing limits. While attending college at the University of Massachusetts in 1992, Amos fell in love with rock climbing, which brought him to northern California and eventually a job packing boxes for Shoreline Mountain Project. While there, Amos helped turn an old school mail-order company into one of the first e-commerce companies, which launched his career into the startup world.

After Shoreline, Amos was either a founder or early employee in six other startups including HotJobs.com, Work.com, Business.com, mySpoonful, BlackLocus, and Joust. At each of these startups, his responsibility was always directly related to figuring out product–market fit, early sales, and building sales organizations. Then, in 2015, he moved over to the investor side as managing director of Techstars in Austin, Texas. Now, after over 70 seed-stage investments, Amos has become one of the most active early-stage investors in all of Texas, via Techstars Austin.

Follow the author on twitter: @iamamoslee

Follow the author on LinkedIn: https://www.linkedin.com /in/amosschwartzfarb/

Email feedback to: amos@sellmorefasterbook.com

Index